**BUILD
LIVE
GIVE**

39 52
code

BUILD
LIVE
GIVE

Growth Drivers to Build your Lifestyle Business

By Paul Higgins

Published by Build Live Give
www.buildlivegive.com
The moral right of the author has been asserted.

For quantity sales or media enquiries, please contact the publisher at the website address above.

Cover design: Julia Kuris
Illustrations: Julia Kuris
Production Consultant: Linda Diggle

ISBN: 978-0-6485264-0-7 (paperback)
         978-0-6485264-1-4 (ebook)

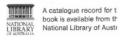 A catalogue record for t
book is available from th
National Library of Austr

Disclaimer
The material in this publication is of the nature of general comment only and does not represent professional advice. It is not intended to provide specific guidance for any particular circumstances and it should not be relied upon for any decision to take action or not to take action on any matter which it covers. The reader should obtain professional advice where appropriate, before making any such decision.

To the maximum extent permitted by law, the author and publisher disclaim all responsibility and liability to any person, arising directly or indirectly from any person taking or not taking action based on the information in this book.

Praise for Build Live Give

'I interview many global entrepreneurs who have made a substantial impact on the world and I often see a common trait – the ability to take action.

Paul Higgins gives solopreneurs a low-risk set of proven actions to achieve success – measured by the lifestyle they want to live. Not everyone is going to build a global unicorn and that is okay.'

Nathan Chan, *CEO of Foundr magazine*

'I speak five languages and love helping entrepreneurs to build lasting relationships which open doors they can only dream of opening. But the language of small business was very foreign to me when I escaped my corporate lawyer's role.

Paul Higgins helps solopreneurs to understand the language of small business so they can leverage their strengths to impact more people in the world.'

Jordan Harbinger,
Critically acclaimed host of the Jordan Harbinger Show

'I admire people who speak from actual experience, instead of just theory. Paul is one of those rare thought leaders who follows this rule. His corporate background, his eventual departure, and the life he has been able to build, for himself and others since, is a testament to his expertise and heart.'

Ari Meisel, *Founder of Less Doing*

'Paul shares a great story about his transition from being an Employee to becoming an Entrepreneur. Remarkably, he has achieved all this whilst living with a major health condition. Inspiring stuff. There are many valuable lessons contained in this book.'

James Schramko,
Author of Work Less, Make More, Founder of SuperFastBusiness.com

'Build Live Give is a wonderful resource for those wanting to build a successful business and create freedom at the same time. Paul weaves in case studies and stories to make this an interesting and actionable book. Must read for solopreneurs!'

Meryl Johnston,
Founder and CEO of Bean Ninjas, Co-Host of the Bean Ninjas Podcast

Dedication

I would like to dedicate this book to two people. One has inspired me all my life and one has been there for me and made one of the most selfless decisions ever.

My mum.

When I was 18, I was diagnosed with an inherited condition called polycystic kidney disease (PKD). The look on my mum's face when she knew it was her genes that would change the course of my life was heartbreaking.

Not for one minute have I ever blamed her. But I know she blames herself and I will probably blame myself when I have to face a similar situation with my children — 50/50 chance at birth! They will not get tested until they are 18.

Mum had complications with her heart as her condition was diagnosed late in life. Somewhat of a family secret, I am afraid. That has all changed now.

Mum went on dialysis in 2009 and went three times a week for five hours at a time. She never complained. Never. She was such a fighter and always put others first.

On the 18th July 2019 she passed away peacefully. My dad, brother and I were by her side.

I am so happy that she lived long enough to see my successful transplant — something she never had the chance to do.

I would like to dedicate this book to her fighting spirit. She modelled how to live with the cards you are dealt.

I see my condition as a blessing. I would most likely still be climbing the corporate ladder without it. I would not have spent quality time with my family, helped hundreds of business owners and survived my recent transplant if not for the tenacity to go above this condition. A gift from her.

Thanks, Mum, for inspiring me to be the best person I can be, to live everyday with joy and to make sure I am giving back.

I will continue your legacy of putting others first and never complaining.

My best mate.

In 1988, I transferred schools for my final year and was mateless. I asked Dad for some golf tickets to buy myself some friends. Shameless, I know, but I was desperate. The first person I handed a ticket to was Brendan Richardson (Richo).

Fast forward to 1999, two days before my wedding. Richo (groomsman) and I are swimming about a kilometre offshore at an iconic Australian beach — Cottesloe in Perth, Western Australia. He mentions he can't make it back and I don't have a backup groomsman (joking), so I get him to shore. He was a little teary and suggested I saved his life at the time — something he refutes today.

We stayed the closest of mates. He is by far a better golfer than I but, as I continually tell him, it was once his career and not mine. For the record, I have beaten him without handicaps a handful of times.

When Linda was ruled out as a donor, Richo said he would give it a go under one condition — I was not allowed to talk about it, make a fuss and cry like a baby in gratefulness. Think of Paul Hogan in *Crocodile Dundee* and you get the picture.

After having more tests than preparing to fly to Mars, the doctors could not believe the match. Many siblings are less compatible. On the 28th of February 2019, it all became a reality. Richo has changed the quality of my life — forever.

Richo was out of the hospital in two days and I was out in four — yes, we are competitive. One of the quickest double escapees acts on record!

What do you say to a mate like this? Well, he is now officially my best mate, if that counts for anything.

The chances of him reading any book, let alone this book, are very slim.

I just want the world to know what a selfless, brave and life-changing act he did. I have made some choices around my health, but many decisions are easy because they are made for me.

Richo had an incredibly hard decision to make and I will forever be grateful.

I believe my other mates, who suggested they would donate, are also very grateful for Richo. In all seriousness, I also want to thank them.

If you are thinking of registering your organs for donation, I strongly encourage you to do so. It has been life-changing for me and for Richo.

TABLE OF CONTENTS

Acknowledgements

I would like to thank my beautiful wife Linda for her support, not just for the book and supporting someone living with a chronic condition, but also her uncompromising passion in backing me through this roller coaster journey. Without her, this would not be possible.

I would like to thank my two gorgeous children, Tamsyn and Liam. They have never complained about the lifestyle adjustments we made as I struggled for many years after leaving my career. They are also my inspiration. I am so proud of the people they have become.

My parents never questioned my ability to live life on my terms. My dad, in particular, helped me make the final leap from my day job to my own business. Without his vision and guidance, I would not be where I am today. Seeing him live with polio all his life and never complaining gave me the optimism and courage to do anything.

To Kathleen Khan, my consulting neurologist, who helped me with kidney failure. She is always there for me and I will be forever grateful.

To all the doctors and nurses who have taken care of me through my journey. There are too many to mention individually, but as a collective, they are truly amazing.

To Kath Walters, my book 'sherpa' — a huge thank you. She gave me the structure, the ease of talking rather than writing and the right amount of challenging me to give you a book which will add value.

Finally, to the Build Live Give community and the thousands of open and brave conversations which formed the practical experiences to make this possible. This also includes my incredible team based in the Philippines and the rich knowledge of experts who support me and my fellow members.

Introduction

This book is the first of three:
BUILD
LIVE
GIVE

At the core of this book is the central theme of building a great business to fund the LIVE and GIVE.

Is life that linear? Never.

So there will be elements of LIVE and GIVE in here for sure. Don't wait for that perfect day or moment. Life can be messy and so are the linkages between BUILD, LIVE, GIVE.

Will you be left with a cliff-hanging moment at the end to make you read the next book?

No. This is not one of those annoying TV shows.

I have written this so you can get 100% value in building your business right now. What I prescribe to BUILD your own business is all here and it comes from practical experience.

I am writing three books because I feel like I have cracked the code on BUILD. I am not where I would like to be on LIVE and GIVE.

Have I fully explored how to take the cash from the business and invest it wisely? Have I found more natural ways to live other than Western medicine? Have I set up my own foundation and cracked the code to make a significant impact?

The short answer is no.

Am I working on it? Yes, and when I've cracked the code like I have for BUILD, I will release the next book.

At the end of this book, I will invite you to follow my journey of writing the next book LIVE. You can get a behind-the-scenes view and learn what it takes to get that book sitting inside of you into the world.

So what will this book cover?

- ▶ How to be more effective with your time and work ON the business
- ▶ How to pick the right clients so you can get referrals and introductions
- ▶ How to structure your business model so you get paid for the value you add
- ▶ How to have people chasing you, rather than the other way around
- ▶ How to build a high-performing team so you can live and give.

This book will give you a proven formula to go from uncertainty to certainty. In short, it is packaged into the Five Rapid Growth Drivers.

1. Personal effectiveness
2. Ideal client
3. Right business model
4. Sales focus
5. High performing team

We will cover these in detail in the following chapters.

Chapter 1
The frying pan moment

Y ou leave the comfort of the crowd and go solo. It may be working in corporate, it may be number two in someone's business, or it may be a vocation. You are tired of being in the shadows and want to step into the spotlight. You want to test yourself while still living the lifestyle you are accustomed to. In the past, you had the money but lacked purpose and lifestyle.

So you left. And now you get the lifestyle benefits, which is fantastic. But after a while, you find the financial side starts to wane. And that creates its own set of worries and challenges.

You worry about your financial security. You go to remortgage — to do anything with your finances — and they ask you about your financial position. And you have little to show when it comes to taxable income. It's challenging. You worry about the lifestyle you're accustomed to, the activities you're used to doing. If you're in a life partnership and you have children, you're accustomed to spending a certain amount of income, leasing the car, everything that came with someone else paying you a wage. And all of a sudden, it is up to you.

It creates some tension. You're used to someone else picking up the bill. Now you don't have the cash flow to pay for it. Yes, you have reserves and a potential inheritance, but that needs to be protected and not relied upon. You are not used to thinking about where the next dollar will come from.

Then the self-doubt sets in. You think this kind of struggle is isolated to you. That's not the case. Most solopreneurs struggle financially. And you have a new pressure: to be all things to all people. When you worked for someone else, your family expected and got used to you being 'missing in action'. Now, your life partner expects you to be there as a partner and a parent, to be more involved than you were, and to still contribute financially. If you have been the key financial contributor, people still expect you to deliver. This is a challenge.

You realise, over time, that you need a new skill set. The skills which brought you success working for someone else are different from the skills you need to be successful on your own. Some of them are applicable, but not all of them.

In my case, I spent 18 years becoming an absolute expert in strategy, sales and leadership. I'd walk in the room and be confident because I knew my stuff. In your own business, you walk into an environment, and you're the least knowledgeable in the room. It is a big change.

There is a benefit to deeply understanding the pain that many of us experience when transitioning. This also carries through to different growth stages in your own business.

That understanding has an impact on both your mental and physical wellbeing. From a mental point of view, it is a rollercoaster, and you can have a lot of self-doubts. Keeping your confidence up is important and keeping the cash coming in helps you to feel more successful. If you are used to success and you're not making the money you're used to, you might feel inadequate or not as confident. It's a big one.

On the physical side, you start to cut corners. I will talk later about the five energy drivers and how they all have to occur at once. The one I will call out here is sleep. Sleep is the best way to 10x your business.

Recognising and getting support for the mental and physical challenges is hard to do.

In this chapter, I will introduce you to the three most common experiences encountered by most transitions and show you how to plot where you are on the path to success. You might feel that everything is roses, in which case I am delighted for you. This book shows you how to capitalise on your success to date. Or you might feel ready to give up and head back to work for someone else. This book will show you how to keep your dream alive and give you a proven framework that gets results.

My transition story

I was in the corporate world for 18 years. I worked for The Coca-Cola Company for my entire corporate career.

I did a double major in accounting and marketing at university back in the '90s, when jobs were hard to come by. I finished university, and there were few job opportunities. I had said I would never work at the company my father worked for, but they said, 'Look, just do a sales job for six months until you find out what you want to do, and it'll be fine.' So I did. They had a 'Top Gun' award, which was for the best salesperson. I won two quarters in a row. Then I got offered an amazing opportunity to become a district sales manager — the youngest in the company, or so I was told!

I moved on to manage the Coles supermarket account nationally at 25. It was brilliant. We came up with the concept of selling cold single-serve products at the front counter in supermarkets, which became a massive profit-driver. I had a great time with some huge wins. From there, I ran some of the world's largest food-service customers.

I loved the diversity of working in a global business while helping large and small businesses. Coca-Cola had a big impact on their profitability. I'd go in as a consultant to understand how their business worked and how I could positively impact it. I had unbelievable access to these business owners and their businesses, and I helped them implement the changes. What I loved with Coca-Cola, in particular, was that it was both strategic and action-oriented.

One minute I was at a board meeting with the CEO, talking about the future of our industry in the next 20 years and on the same day we would go out to customers and take action — 'What does this outlet look like?' 'Has it got the right standards and is everything looking right?'

The seeds of change

But in the background, I was a ticking time bomb. I had an inherited condition called Polycystic Kidney Disease (PKD), which I touched on earlier. At one point, my specialist said, 'If you continue to work the hours with the stress and the travel, you're going to have kidney failure in 12 to 24 months.' At that time, there were no living donor options on the table, and I would have a minimum of a six-year wait for a transplant.

She said the alternative was to change my environment and my stress levels, and that I could then prolong the life of your kidney for another five or more years. She couldn't predict exactly how the disease was going to develop, but she knew for sure that I had to change my work life.

It was a sobering moment. I told her I wanted to beat the odds and get eight or nine more years. (Yes, I am competitive.)

My father-in-law was then diagnosed with cancer. I went back to Perth and ran the Coca-Cola Perth sales team to be closer to him. My family values took a stronger hold from living through this experience.

Within six months, the powers that be said, 'Look, you're doing a great job, but Western Australia is only a tenth of the total Australian volume, and we want you back in the big game.'

I became an intrapreneur in the company. They had a problem with juice because it was a market where we had a low share compared to other categories. I took the juice business from low nine figures to high nine figures in two years with the help of a passionate team. It was effectively a startup success.

We extended an iconic Australian brand called Golden Valley into juice, bought some other businesses with cold juice capability and launched across Australia. We had an innovative distribution system where we put cold products on the back of non-refrigerated trucks. This utilised one of our greatest assets and made it economical to have cold-chain products.

This was a world-first, and the heads of Coca-Cola in other countries took our innovation back to their markets.

On my own time, I worked on small business boards to understand how they ticked. The more I did, the more I realised that at some point I'd love to go and run my own business. I set a goal to learn as much as I could to prepare for success — a long-term play.

Then the goalposts moved. My father used to say, 'Every corporate person has a number. At the end of the day, you're just a number, and your number will come up one day. That happens in the corporate world. It's not about you. It's not personal.' His words rang true in my ears when I was offered a promotion one night in 2011, and then the next day, it was taken back. They said, 'Now you've got to go apply for the role, or you can patiently wait until we find you a role.' I asked for a redundancy. They unofficially implied I was too good to be made redundant, so I had to stay even if it wasn't something I loved to do. I felt betrayed. Then I remember what my father had said.

I also felt a personal conflict working at Coca-Cola while battling with kidney disease. Sugar is one of the biggest causes of diabetes and diabetes leads to kidney failure. Approximately 30% of patients on dialysis have diabetes. That is not the way it happened in my case, but I did feel slightly compromised. I loved my time at Coca-Cola and will always be grateful for the opportunities they gave me. In saying that, their core products contain high amounts of sugar and impact the health of consumers all over the planet. It is always the consumer's choice, but I felt a conflict with my core values to leave a positive legacy in the world. I felt like the product, and the company I worked for didn't completely align with my beliefs and values. This is a personal view and one I don't express often.

I had a daily reflection, a mission statement, where I read about the person I wanted to be and the impact I wanted to have in the world. Then I went and behaved in a different way at work. It just didn't feel congruent to who I wanted to be. I was living a double life, and it was tiring. It was up to me to make a change. So I resigned.

A euphoric start

I felt euphoric at the start. It was a huge burst of freedom to create something brand new. I had to create a new name for my company, a new website. A whole lot of learning came about, which was fantastic. I talked to new people about what I was doing, and I loved it. I could see the benefits instantly. It was like I was a new person.

In many ways, I didn't realise how good The Coca-Cola Company was until I left and worked as a consultant to other global brands.

I trained with FranklinCovey, the world's number one productivity training company. I had followed Steven Covey since '91 when I first read *The 7 Habits of Highly Effective People*. I'd put all my team through FranklinCovey courses. They were the values and the principles I lived by. In the end, I realised that working with another provider was not going to make the money I needed, even though I loved the work.

I also coached and mentored small business owners and corporate executives. It was fantastic. I loved the freedom, travelling the world, meeting people and also spending more time with my family, which was my number one purpose.

In the first 12 months, it was great. I didn't realise how stressed, how angry, and how aloof I was with my family or how disconnected I was from my children until I started to get back into their world.

The shine wears off

Then I looked at the scoreboard. At Coca-Cola, we were results-oriented — it was in their DNA. I didn't want to lose that ability. In the first 12 months, I did.

I threw a lot of the principles I'd used in my past life out the window because I had all this newfound freedom. Then I realised I wasn't hitting my numbers. I had lots of conversations with potential clients that went nowhere. I chased the wrong clients. I thought anyone with a heartbeat was a potential client. I did too many of the wrong things, which meant I didn't get a result. Around that time I went to remortgage our house and the bank said, 'Well, where're your last three years of income?' I'm like, 'There are none.' I had all the excuses in the world — but, deep down, I realised I didn't have a working formula.

Linda and I had agreed to cash in the bank figure each month. I was giving her doom and gloom instead. She said, 'Look, I am here to support you, and I love how you are supporting us around the house, but I am also worried about our financials. We planned to build a new house and right now I don't think we can.'

Linda felt more pressure to continue to work in a job and an environment she didn't love. That pressure started to get to me. I thought I was letting my family down.

I was trading time for money. I found it hard to get new clients, and I was balancing sales and delivery. I ran out of capacity. I ran out of hours to work. I was back to working corporate hours plus some. I worked on weekends, which I had promised never to do. I was with my kids when I needed to be, but at night, when everyone went to sleep, I worked. My health was also impacted. My blood pressure was rising, and my kidney function was falling.

I wanted to sort this out myself. I had put myself in this situation, and I needed to get myself out. Like in a job, the harder you work, the more success you get. Toughen up, as my old boss used to say. But I realised there was more to it than that. The lessons I learned are all contained in this book.

From euphoria...

So I went from cycling in the Dandenongs (hilly part of Melbourne, Australia), listening to a podcast during the middle of the day to a crisis point.

...to identity crisis...

I would walk into a networking event and not be able to describe what I did. If someone asked me, 'Paul, who are you, and what do you do?' I couldn't answer. I felt enormous pressure. At family events, everyone would say, 'How's it going?' I'd say, 'Yeah, it's fantastic. It's going well. And they would ask, 'So what do you do?' I just made it up. It was a different answer every time. With simple things like what to write on my LinkedIn profile, I constantly changed the message and who I wanted to target.

In social media, you see endless success stories. People constantly talk about the success they've had. Some of it is true, but a lot isn't when you dig behind the scenes. That is a problem because people get a false idea of what it takes to get it right. You think it'll happen overnight. That's not always the case.

...to panic

The third phase was a panic. As I mentioned before, the numbers were bad. Each quarter's government bill, I was struggling to pay. I had to ask for an extension. I know a lot of people do. The Australian tax department, even though they get a bad rap, are quite good. But all those things meant I started to hit the panic button. Also, you cannot borrow money when you have a government tax debt.

I faced a unique problem at the panic stage. This is when most people would say, 'Well, look. I'll go back to working for someone. This is all too hard.' But for me, with my declining kidney function, going back to working for someone was problematic. I had to try to figure it out.

People might say, 'Well if you've got the lifestyle you want, why is money important?' That is the choice you made, isn't it? Lifestyle over money.' I agree: money isn't the be-all and end-all. But you're used to contributing to the daily budget or the daily household maintenance. You want to be able to go on family holidays without worrying if it will be eating into your savings.

Some people say, 'Look, it doesn't matter about the money. If you're passionate about what you do, the money will come.'

What I learnt is that this is not always the case. The pressure of not earning an income will impact your motivation and self-worth. It doesn't matter how resilient you are. If you don't get help, and you don't have the right mentoring to get a balance of lifestyle and finances, it can take a lot longer for you to have true freedom.

SUGGESTION: You might be saying 'Well if it is all that hard, why don't I just quit and give up now?' And this is a fair point. But most benefits in life come with struggles. You can do it all alone and take too much time to work it out as I did, or you can learn from others and be supported and reduce the time it takes. Find out more at www.buildlivegive.com

Summary

Think of a simple set of scales. Working for someone — you have the finances, but you don't have the flexibility, lifestyle and responsibility. That flips when you run your own business.

Solopreneurship is a rollercoaster. You're going to have your good days, and you're going to have your bad days. You need people around you to help you work through it. They say you can't have your cake and eat it too, but you can. You can have a brilliant lifestyle, do what you love and also have the financial security you've always deserved.

Instead of taking five years, as I did, and making all the same mistakes many before you have made, you can get to financial success faster. And as mentioned before, financial success is only a way of funding what you really want to do. In the next two unpublished books, we will cover LIVE and GIVE in more detail.

If you follow the steps in this book, it may take you less time to build your own successful business, no matter what your base is now.

You might be wondering how you can follow this program. If you had more time, then, of course, you could do everything I am going to tell you.

In the next chapter, I am going to stop time from being the issue. The first step of my solution is to win you back the time you need to make changes.

Chapter 2
Time is not the problem

Personal effectiveness is my field — my personal passion. I am an expert in effectively using time. But there is something strange about the effectiveness issue. I found that even when I used my time well, I still didn't get the results I needed.

In this chapter, I'm going to prove that time is not the problem. What you spend it on is the problem.

You don't need more hours, but you do need to use them wisely. Putting time into working ON your business will get you results.

Gary Vaynerchuk (Gary V) talks about the hustle. If you are building a global brand like his, then maybe, yes. But if you are building a business to fund your lifestyle and to GIVE, then I don't totally agree. I did write a LinkedIn post about this and got a personal message back from Gary. The media do take his comments to the extreme, but he is definitely not a 30-40 hours a week kind of guy.

There are many experts spruiking all kinds of shiny objects. Everyone's in a sea of exhaustion, trying to do all these things. Then you say to yourself, 'Well, hang on. I can't do all those things. I don't have time to do everything. I need to make distinct choices around what I will do.'

Breaking the $20,000-a-month revenue barrier

How do you make these choices? Well, I've saved you the trouble of choosing because I've done everything that you're NOT meant to do.

My Five Rapid Growth Drivers (5RGD) are back-engineered to grow a high 6-7 figure business. In other words, I didn't do the 5RGDs I am about to share with you, and what was the result? It took me a lot longer to get to where I needed to be. I can tell you from personal experience that if you do these 5RGDs, then you will avoid some of the difficult conversations I had with my partner.

While you're growing your own business, revenue is typical $5,000-15,000 a month — this is OK. What I will give you is a proven approach to get you to $20,000+ a month.

Is it a guarantee? No. You have to do the work and, most importantly, be prepared to let go of what is not making you successful today.

Once you get to about $20,000 a month, you've solved many cash flow problems. You can pay a remote team to help you, you can pay yourself, and you've got money to invest in marketing for growth. In many service businesses with under $20,000 in monthly revenue, you struggle between sales and delivery. So you think, 'Well if I just had more time to work harder I could make my way out of this.'

Personal effectiveness is about what you say NO to

The distinction I am making here is to say that time is not the problem. If time were the problem, I would have been an instant millionaire. I am an effectiveness expert. I spend my time effectively, and I always have. The problem we all face is how to spend our time on the right things.

When people are working for someone else, time is always pressing on them. They're short on time, but they are typically reactive. Everyone else is controlling their agenda.

When you leave to run your own business, it flips. All of a sudden, you've got plenty of time and no one pressing your agenda. The mistake most people make — like me — is to fill that time with lots of activities. We think that the harder we work, the more successful we will be.

Work on the right activities at the right time. That is the essence. It's not about more hours in the day.

If I were to interview a business expert today on my podcast about how to grow my business, I would get varying opinions. Many experts sadly focus on selling you a program and not on getting you a result.

Has this happened to you? It's happened to me several times. I invested around USD$15,000 in an online course creator. They took me through a structure, and nothing ever eventuated. They disappeared. I never launched my course. I was left embarrassed and my profit for the year was gone. Was it all their fault? Not completely. I didn't ask the right questions.

It wasn't just the profit; it was the time I invested.

Many solopreneurs get led down 'dead-ends' unwittingly. Many are marketing-related. There are also many business coaches out there doing similar things. Many are good, however, are sadly in it for themselves.

Your time is your most valuable asset

The 5RGDs involve little or no expense with external providers. I have invested hundreds of thousands of dollars for you already! Implementing the 5RGDs will require time.

Many solopreneurs don't value their time. When you worked for someone else, time was rarely tracked. Your salary was not linked to time or, in many cases, results.

In your own business, you think, 'Well, money's not coming in, and I'm a free resource. I'll keep doing everything myself.' Your time is worth money and I strongly recommend you look at an effective hourly rate model.

Here are some typical traps of using your 'free' time:

i. Administration

You do your accounts and organise your meetings. You write emails and do your quotes. You become the procurement department for your business — so you research a lot. You set up banking and organise phones and computers. Do you want a post office box or to use your home address? Do you buy a printer? Should it be colour? You face a whole host of decisions you have never confronted before. They're not huge strategic decisions, but they take time. There are a million administrative tasks that used to be done by your team. Now you're doing it all.

ii. Meetings without a clear intent

In my experience, many meetings don't lead anywhere. A common mistake is not to set up the real reason why you want to meet people. Without this, and even with good intent from both sides, it doesn't turn into any business. You have many coffees, many face-to-face meetings, yet your bank account keeps going down.

iii. Face-to-face meetings

I'm still amazed at how many people say, 'I want to meet you in person.' It's nice to meet somebody, but it's not essential, and it takes time to drive there, get parking, etc. When you are an employee, you are getting paid, so it wasn't as noticeable. But when it's your business, and there's no revenue coming in, the cost becomes more apparent.

iv. Free webinars

Just when you are thinking, 'What am I going to do?' an email about a webinar comes into your inbox. Great copywriters tell you this will solve all your worries. 'Watch this 45-minute webinar, and your life's problems will be solved. Here are the examples of how we've done it before.' It's a slick marketing machine, but you get on the webinar , and you can't use most of the content. It is all feathers and no chicken. You wasted your time on it, and then at the end, they try to upsell you into a paid program. The webinar is a tripwire to get you into their paid plan. Beware.

I've spoken to many people who have watched these webinars, trying to find the silver bullet. I did so too. I put it down as market research time, but it was the time I could have better spent discovering the critical problems of my ideal clients, solving those problems and getting paid for it. That would have been far better than trying to look for the elusive silver bullet.

v. Social media

When you're not feeling great, and you haven't quite found the solutions you need, you might think, *'Well, I'll go and spend a couple of minutes on social media to see if anything pops up. I'll flick onto my Facebook. LinkedIn, Twitter or Instagram.'* Then you're consuming content. Some are valuable, but it's the 80/20 rule where 80% of it is noise and is not going to help you. When I get my clients to track their time, they usually find social media is a huge time-waster. Apple's IOS now helps you track your screen time. Did you get a shock? Or are you too scared to look?

vi. Emails

We all know the dangers of spending time in your inbox. Later in this book, I'm going to show you how you can set up for zero time in your inbox, so you never have to visit it again! But when you are surrounded by things not going your way, people love to search for good news. You pop in and have a look at your inbox. Half an hour or 45 minutes later, you find you have read stuff that isn't adding any value. It is so easy to get lost in your inbox. You can sometimes find bad news instead.

vii. Delivery

I am going to sound crazy, but delivery is a common distraction for service-based business owners. That is because to build, live and give, you must sell AND manage capacity. My clients say, 'You know, I'm just so busy doing delivery.' But their rates are low. They need some cash in the door or the scope of the project 'bleeds', and they are doing more than they were paid for. That takes time away from sales, and it becomes a vicious cycle.

A friend spent ten months pitching for a $75,000 contract. It fell through. It turns out she had done ten months of work without pay. She wanted to close her business down when that happened. Some people will take as much of your intellectual property as they can get without paying you. And if you're a giving person, it's pretty easy to be taken advantage of in this way. Most of us look at the upside. We say to ourselves, 'What this client promised me would come off.' Unfortunately, it's the other way around: 20% of what's promised comes off, not 80%.

Whole days can disappear

There are some common uses of time you can quickly fall into if you don't have the right structure. It's like the old saying: 'Moving deck chairs on the Titanic.' You are busy. Your life partner walks in, and you say, 'Yeah, I worked for 10 hours today.' But it's a lot harder to quantify the results. The results aren't direct. You are building trust that leads to future sales. It's a bit ambiguous.

When you worked for someone, it wasn't as easy to measure cause and effect, but somehow you got paid. In your own business, it doesn't work that way. You get on a sales call because you need the sales — but without the right process, you don't realise what your buyer wants. There's a truism on social media that says only 3% of people you interact with are ready to buy. How do you work out who is in the 3%? If you don't, you will waste time on prospects not ready to buy right now.

Don't waste another minute on the wrong tasks

Do any of these distractions sound familiar to you? I've written about some of the typical time wasters, but you might have more. It's time to put an end to this and refocus on building your own business to fund living and giving back. In the next chapter, I'll show you how to use your time effectively to allow you do focus on the other four RGDs.

I'll show you how you can use technology and outsourcing to remove some administration and delivery tasks. I'll reveal how to pick the right amount of administrative support for your stage of growth. You will start with the right expert, so you're not rehiring down the track. Some people try to find the cheapest person online. Often the person is great at the start, but finds it hard to balance demand and can disappear. You then have to rehire and retrain. This costs you both time and money.

Remember, if you were buying and starting a franchise business, you would borrow money to set it up. You will need to kick in a little bit of money to set up. The trick is spending it on the right things.

Support your most expensive and valuable resource

So many of us discount our own time and consider ourselves the cheapest resource in our service-based business. In fact, we are the most expensive resource in our service-based business. We've got an excellent methodology to get the support you need quickly, and it all starts with personal effectiveness.

Summary

We have discussed that time is not the problem. It is what you do with your time which is the problem.

Avoid some of the common time wasters of:
- Administration tasks
- Unnecessary meeting — especially face to face
- Attending free webinars
- Burying yourself in social media.

The key action from this chapter is to ask people who you know and trust what they observe in you that you may not see in yourself.

Take this advice and see what you can eliminate to gain some time, then use it wisely in the implementing actions from upcoming chapters.

In the next chapter, we will give you some brilliant tips on how to be more effective with the activities that are needed in business but necessarily needed to be done by you.

Chapter 3

Rapid Growth Driver 1 — Personal Effectiveness

Right now, you are very busy wearing many hats.

I want to help you to divert your time to the most important, non-urgent at the expense of urgent and unimportant. How can I do this? By combining:

1. You

2. Us

3. Personal systems

This is not a false promise. What I suggest in this chapter are tangible and easy-to-achieve actions that you can implement to direct your time wisely.

This is the time you will use to change and to do work on the big-ticket items.

When we run into the problems I've outlined in Chapters 1 and 2, we often pressure ourselves by thinking, '*Should I go and work for someone else?*' followed by, '*Do I go and get a part-time job to supplement some of my income? Do I go and work full-time and then run my business as more of a side hustle?*'

And then it's a slippery slope back to the memories of working for someone. Here is the horrible truth: once you have been your own boss, you realise that working for someone else is not a world you want to go back to. You're stuck — you can't go forward, and you can't go back. Then you think, '*I've got to change, I've got to do something different.*'

The most important change you can make is to be more effective with your time.

Meet Pollyanna

Pollyanna Lenkic is a thought leader in the field of high-performing teams, based in Melbourne, Australia. She has run and then sold, an incredibly successful business in the United Kingdom where she built a business from start-up to an £11 million turnover. She is a super-smart person with a lot of business experience, wisdom and a truly giving nature.

But when she decided to start coaching, she needed a whole new set of business tools. She wasn't the head of a large company; she was a solopreneur. She knew she needed a remote team and a bunch of effectiveness tools to run her practice, but she didn't know where to start.

She had also gotten comfortable with doing things herself. It was 'quicker' just to do everything herself and the cost of this was working many hours.

My first suggestion to Pollyanna was to get a Virtual Assistant (VA). She had two attempts at it. With the first attempt, she was not ready. The second time worked out extremely well. Why the difference? A key difference Pollyanna shared with me was that with the second time, she dedicated her time to investing in the partnership and getting some help.

The first time, Pollyanna didn't have the technology set up and was so busy delivering amazing value to her clients she didn't have the capacity to train a VA. With the second time, we helped Pollyanna recruit and train a VA. We put together a technology stack that was simple to use and, most importantly, we trained Pollyanna. In my seven years of running a VA company, it was often the client who was underprepared. VAs, especially from the Philippines, tend to be career VAs. They have worked with many solopreneurs and entrepreneurs from around the globe. However, like Pollyanna, until they experienced it firsthand, they found the learning curve too steep.

Now Pollyanna is creating amazing content with her newfound freedo. She has more time to deliver what she loves, but she's using technol. her VA to be able to connect with more clients. As a result, he thriving.

You

The noise of running your own business can be overwhelming. If you allow it to, it can totally absorb your life. You can quickly spiral into a state of overwhelm and task overload. When you had a job, you could rely on others to help you when you felt this way. Now all trains are headed to your platform, and you simply can't get all the passengers off in time. This congestion leads to poor health — both physical and mental — and also poor decision-making.

Now I will take you through four habits which, when followed, will help you to be the best version of you possible.

Energy

As stated in Chapter 1, I helped to launch FranklinCovey's *The 5 Choices to Extraordinary Productivity* in the Asia-Pacific region. The fifth choice was called 'Fuel Your Fire, Don't Burn Out'. While I saw the sense in having it as number five, I believe it should come first.

As James Schramko from Super Fast Business says, 'A healthy owner has a healthy business.'

So what are the five, and how can you take action?

re fortunate to work from home in some of the most
planet. With freedom comes responsibility. You were
r — not anymore. So it is time to MOVE. According
ink 7% better on your feet.

Take a phone call. You typically will stand up and start walking around whilst you are talking.

What your version of the move is specific to you and your circumstances. For me, with the restrictions post-transplant, it is walking my dog, taking the stairs and going for a walk with my wife. I hope to be back to golf and tennis soon.

EAT

I am sure you are aware of the correlation between what you eat and how you think. Some simple tips:

▶ Eat high-quality proteins for breakfast

▶ Avoid high sugar and eat high glucose and high fibre

▶ Approximately 80% of your brain is made up of water and good fats which you need to replenish constantly

▶ Eat from the rainbow — different coloured vegetables and fruits.

SLEEP

The number one question a physician or general practice doctor should ask you is: 'How many quality hours of sleep are you getting a night.'

The number and what is classified as the quality is up for debate. As a guide, seven hours a night is something to aim for.

Think of it like defragging your hard drive. You need sleep to clear your RAM, ready for the next day.

Some simple tips:

▶ No screen time 30 minutes prior to bed

▶ No digital devices in the bedroom

▶ Warm shower prior to bed

▶ Blockout blinds on windows.

RELAX

Relaxing and solopreneurship normally don't go in the same sentence. As discussed before, there is unending pressure to be busy. If you don't do it, who will? It is easy to fall into a pattern of always being on.

Some simple tips:

- ▶ Remove the negative self-talk — write down your negative thoughts on a piece of paper and throw it in the bin
- ▶ Deep breathing — breathe in through your nose and count to five, then exhale for five (I do this at the end of a 30-minute work block)
- ▶ Eating the right diet, as per above, and taking omega 3 and vitamin D supplements.

CONNECT

In a fast-paced digital world, it is important to take the time to have human-to-human interactions and connections in a physical environment. Think back to the last truly engaging conversation you had with someone. How did you feel at the end? You probably felt energised, alive and refreshed.

Some simple tips:

- ▶ Have good eye contact with people (culturally appropriate)
- ▶ Go on walks with people
- ▶ Play sports
- ▶ Have good old-fashioned dinner parties

The key to maintaining high energy is to do all five at once. FranklinCovey called it 'patterns of consistent renewal'.

As part of onboarding to our membership and masterminds, we ask people to rate themselves out of seven points on each of the five energy drivers. It is rare for someone to be doing all five above seven points.

Mindfulness

Your greatest asset is your mind. You want it to be in peak condition to be able to share your knowledge and wisdom with others and help them to achieve their results. I will not go down a rabbit hole here.

Some books I recommend to read on the topic are:

- *Psychological Types* by Carl Jung
- *Deep Work* by Cal Newport
- *Turning Pro: Tap Your Inner Power and Create Your Life's Work* by Steven Pressfield

A way of doing this is working in a state of 'flow'.

According to Wikipedia, positive psychology, a flow state, is the mental state of operation in which a person performing an activity is fully immersed in a feeling of energized focus, full involvement, and enjoyment in the process of the activity. In essence, flow is characterized by complete absorption in what one does, and a resulting loss in one's sense of space and time.

Named by Mihály Csíkszentmihályi in 1975, the concept has been widely referred to across a variety of fields (and is particularly well recognized in occupational therapy), though the concept has existed for thousands of years under other names, notably in some Eastern religions, for example, Buddhism.

One way of increasing your ability to work in a state of flow is through meditation.

Which meditation technique best suits you is often an exercise in experimentation.

I personally find the Headspace app[1] is a good place to start. I do 10 minutes every night.

---

1 https://www.headspace.com/

...er of focusing on what you can control and not wasting time thinking about the results.

Anyone can have a goal of making it to the Olympics. This is the easy part. The harder part is working through the repetition of training and daily habits, which will see the goal achieved.

In *Atomic Habits* by James Clear[1], he talks about how the difference between a highly successful athlete and the rest of us is their ability to turn up to training on the days they least feel like it and be able to cope with the boredom of repetitive training (habits).

This translates into running your own business. I have released a podcast every week for over two years, whilst being on dialysis, having three major operations and spending more days in hospital than I would like to remember. It was a habit I knew would bring me success if I was consistent at it.

I use an app called Super Habit[2] on my iPhone and also recommend Way of Life[3] for Android. I would recommend searching for habit trackers in the future, as this is an evolving space.

The key habits I track daily are:
- ▶ Morning routine
- ▶ Focus on my One Thing[4]
- ▶ Five energy drivers
- ▶ Sales
- ▶ Clients
- ▶ Give gratitude

---

1   https://jamesclear.com/atomic-habits
2   https://www.superhabit.co
3   https://wayoflifeapp.com/
4   https://www.the1thing.com/

- Research
- Daily progress journal
- Meditation
- Record a video

My habits will not necessarily be the right ones for you. What is important is doing them consistently. I find an accountability partner helps with this.

My 17-year-old daughter is doing her final year of school as I am writing this book. She inherited my ability to dream. We discussed how we both want the outcome without loving the work. I read her parts of James Clear's book, and we agreed to use the Super Habit app and hold each other accountable. It is working really well.

We use the same concept in our masterminds. You have both group and paired accountability.

Under the morning routine component of the habit tracker, I do the following activities:

- Three daily priorities
- Daily reflection (http://buildlivegive.com/book-resources)

At night I do the progress journal:

- Biggest win
- Key challenge
- Gratitude

Time blocking

You will already know when you are likely to be in the focus state. Some will be in the morning, like me, and some will be at night. The time of day is less important. What is more important is what you do within the focus window.

The hardest part about doing this is just that — doing it. The concept is very simple.

Look at the first item on your list of the three most important tasks and focus on it, and it only, for 30 minutes. I time it on my iPhone. Block everything else out.

When the alarm goes off, then have a 2-minute break. Breathe, as mentioned in the relax section, have a drink of water and walk around. I go up and down my staircase. I also swap from sitting to standing for the next block and using my standup desk.

I do this for 3-4 blocks in a row.

I have my team monitoring my emails, social platforms and anything else deemed as a distraction.

Would I be able to run my business, build a new house and write this book while managing my health? Possible, but unlikely.

If you are like most solopreneurs who work for themselves and enjoy the freedom, you probably have a little voice going inside your head — 'I could never be that disciplined'. I get it, I've felt the same.

After getting over myself and removing the excuses, I did it, and it was the single biggest action that moved the needle for me. It may not be for you, but don't die wondering.

I work with my clients to come up with their Core Four — the four activities only they can do — and then have them spend 80% of their time on them. We track this using Toggl[1] and report on it weekly.

---

1   https://toggl.com/

For example, it could be sales, marketing, client delivery and research. Your time blocking should mirror which four tasks are the most important to you.

Us

As I mentioned previously, being a solopreneur does not mean you have to do everything yourself.

You might be the only person who can come up with your unique intellectual property (IP), sell it and deliver components of it. However, there are many other components to running your own business which you can get help with.

At the same time, it doesn't mean you have to have full-time roles where there is the risk of under capacity.

The rise in the gig economy (independent workers for short-term engagements) in corporates is mirrored by the rise of the freelance economy.

You can tap into specific expertise to fill the tasks you are not good at, don't like to do or are taking your focus from what you do best.

I call it the Plus One effect — you are the solopreneur, and then you bring in an expert to compliment you and achieve more than either of you could apart.

There are four elements to getting this right:
1. Personality profiling
2. Virtual Assistants
3. Experts
4. Routines

We will cover each here.

Personality profiling

To be who you are today, you have inherited certain genetics, lived specific experiences and acquired specific skills. This is individual to you and influences the way you see the world.

This is the same for the people you work and collaborate with. In a previous life, you might have leveraged your position to influence them. Now you have to win their hearts and minds as, in many cases, you are not the only person they are working for.

So how do you know the best way to work with someone? If you are like the majority of the population, you guess and then default to your natural style. The short-term gain can mask the longer-term issue of low engagement and loyalty.

The best managers in the game take time to understand the other person's point of view and tailor their approach to leverage strengths.

One way is to ask them some open questions like:

1. How do you like to work?
2. How do you like to communicate?
3. Who has been the best person to work for and why?
4. Who has been the person you least liked to work for and why?

Another way is to use some personality profiling tools. There are several free and paid options.

Free:

▶ DISC[1]

▶ Personality assessor[2]

---

1   https://www.tonyrobbins.com/disc/
2   https://www.personalityassessor.com/bigfive/

- 16 Personalities[3]
- VIA Institute on Character[4]

Paid:

- Gallup's CliftonStrengths 34[5]
- Strengthscope[6]
- Herrmann Brain Dominance Instrument[7]

Provide a free or paid profiling tool for them and ask them to interpret their results. I am qualified in DISC and HBDI. I recommend that, if you are going to spend thousands of dollars on leveraging the person's experience, you invest in getting a professional to debrief them.

Virtual Assistants

I believe there are three essentials to running your own business

1. Mobile phone
2. Computer/tablet
3. Virtual Assistants

I have dedicated the next chapter to leveraging a virtual assistant.

---

3   https://www.16personalities.com/
4   https://www.viacharacter.org/
5   https://www.gallupstrengthscenter.com/
6   https://www.strengthscope.com/
7   https://www.herrmann.com.au/hbdi-and-programs/

Experts

Many solopreneurs overestimate their own ability. There are times when it is a benefit to learn something first and then hand it over to someone else. Some examples might include:

- ▸ LinkedIn posting
- ▸ LinkedIn messaging
- ▸ Sales follow-up
- ▸ Client onboarding
- ▸ Sales Navigator
- ▸ Project Management
- ▸ Standard Operating Procedures
- ▸ Checklists
- ▸ Social posting

These aren't in your wheelhouse, but they are tasks you have the skills to do, and you would like to customise first.

However, there are some tasks which you may not have the skills for and taking time to learn and apply them can cost you time and money.

Some examples may include:

- ▸ Graphic design
- ▸ Web development
- ▸ Bookkeeping
- ▸ Paid ads
- ▸ Accounting
- ▸ Legal
- ▸ Automation
- ▸ Content writing
- ▸ Podcast editing
- ▸ Book publishing

This is where you need to get experts to help you.

The sources are varied as to where you can find the best experts. Some that work well for solopreneurs are:

- Referrals from peers
- Posting in social media
- Referrals from communities you belong to
- Searching on marketplaces, e.g. Expert360[1] and Clarity.fm

The questions I recommend you ask are:

- What is unique about what you do?
- Who is your ideal client?
- How does it work if I was to become a client?
- What is the investment?
- What guarantees do you provide?
- What social proof do you have?

Then based on the answers, get them to do a paid test. Break it down to one simple task and then assess their abilities compared to other people you have used in the past.

Look for the little things when working with them. Do they communicate well? Do they meet deadlines? Do they deliver on the requirements of what you've asked?

Expect that you will make some mistakes and get some valuable learnings from this. It has taken me over nine years to perfect my process, which I now provide to our community members at www.buildlivegive.com.

We have taken the hard work out of it for you. We have compiled over 300 experts across 150 categories.

Our process is for the team to research an expert and do desktop analysis. If they pass, I then have a meeting with them to determine if we move to

---

1   https://expert360.com/

a trial with one of our members. In this call, I also find out if our members match their ideal client profile.

Then we do the trial, and the member gives a net promoter score (NPS) between 1 and 10 (10 highest) at the end of the trial and a recommendation on whether the community should use this expert in the future.

Ongoing, we do an NPS score after each engagement. If the score is above 7, no action taken. If the score is below 7, then we investigate. If the expert is deemed not to be a good fit, we take them off the list.

You can get immediate access to our experts by joining our community at https://buildlivegive.com/more-leads

Routines

As you build your team, you benefit greatly from having set routines which help you to be efficient with your time and not feel like you are creating a rod for your own back.

You started this journey of building your own business not to have a huge team. You wish to leverage your expertise and tap into others. Having the right routines in place allows you to have this excellent balance.

The key here is to delegate, not abdicate. Just because you're tapping into an expert, you should not completely rely on them, and you do need to keep on track with what they are doing. Ultimately, you are a business owner, and you have the final say and final responsibility to get it right.

Some of the key routines I recommend are:

- ▶ Work in progress (WIP) meetings
- ▶ Huddles

You can probably remember, from working in a job, what a work in progress meeting is all about. You may have had bosses that ran great WIPs and also the opposite.

My WIPs typically cover:

- ▶ Actions from last WIP
- ▶ Standard agenda items
- ▶ New discussions
- ▶ Personal development
- ▶ Commitments for next time

I use Asana to help me manage this. Asana will be mentioned in the next section.

Go to Build Live Give Tech https://buildlivegive.com/book-resources to access our templates.

One key tip is to avoid sending lots of short communications through instant message when they are best to be discussed over a video call. As you think of it, put it into the WIP, and you will not have to remember to raise it.

Huddles are a great way of getting immediate updates on a project and feedback on how you can help the team. I typically start with weekly updates and move towards daily as the project is nearing to go live, but it will depend on where the project is at.

The simple structure I use is:

- ▶ What is your biggest win?
- ▶ What is your key learning?
- ▶ What is your capacity out of 10?
- ▶ What is one thing I can help you with right now?

I will discuss further routines in Chapter 8: High performing teams.

Personal systems

Tapping into Virtual Assistants and experts is made easier if you have the right personal systems in place.

What I mean by personal systems is the platform, people and process. I will mainly focus on the platform in this section. Another way of saying the platform is technology. It is fair to say the word technology spooks many people.

In most cases, you'll never get to meet your Virtual Assistant or expert in person. All communication is done online.

Personal systems bridge the gap. In my experience, having a VA will not work without the right personal systems.

Artificial intelligence will eventually replace a lot of what humans do, but I predict it's still a long way off. Voice-to-text, like Siri and Google Assistant, is getting better and better and voice activation, like Google Home and Amazon Echo, is improving rapidly.

Will it be fast enough to replace a human assistant? Time will tell. It is like fully autonomous cars. The closer to launch, the less bullish the timeline.

The great thing is you don't need to be an IT expert to get the benefits. Most of the platforms are user-friendly — not like Microsoft back in the good old days! I have heard they have lifted their game, but my scars run deep.

Of course, everyone has a different level of competence when it comes to platforms.

In the Build Live Give community, we always start with an assessment of where you're at and meet you there. It is a journey, and the most important point is getting on the right highway. You don't want to be the personal systems equivalent of Blockbusters — caught out by technology and in the same breath, overwhelmed by too much technology.

The platforms you need to run your own business

Unless otherwise stated, I am personally using all of the platforms recommended.

I'll reveal the principles I used to pick a platform so that you can make your own informed assessment and decision.

i. Task managers

A task manager is online software that you can access from any device in a structured way to manage your projects and tasks.

Some people like to put tasks in an electronic diary, e.g. Google Calendar. When I trained at FranklinCovey[1], their neurological research indicated this was inefficient.

The other place tasks normally sit in your email inbox. As we talked about in Chapter 2, if you're constantly in your inbox, you're getting distracted. A task manager prevents you from looking at emails. Few people can be disciplined enough to go into email, do a task and get out without getting distracted. If you are in the minority, well done.

The structure can also be a problem. Everyone has a different way of wording things and therefore, important information can be scattered throughout the email body and often missed. A task manager simplifies this with defined fields to fill out.

---

1   https://www.franklincovey.com

For example: if I had 100 people write an email, not everyone would put a due date, the priority level of the task and allocate to the person who's ultimately responsible. A task manager makes that easy to do.

You can also link the documents to specific tasks. This can save people wasting time trying to find things. It's all in the one spot. Because the updates are live, everyone involved can keep an eye on the project, so this also leads to fewer meetings.

i.i. Repeating items

If there's something you've got to do on a regular basis, you don't have to remember it. Humans aren't robots. We're open to missing things. Having a repeating task already set up in your task list makes life a lot easier.

I also use a task manager to capture non-urgent and important items and then assign them to the specific client and project in preparation for the next meeting. I don't have to try to remember it, it is easy to recall in the next meeting, and it allows you to talk about the task with context. Then you can effectively delegate it, rather than just sending another email. Features such as chat sections, attachments and the structure of information will improve effectiveness.

While message platforms like Slack, WhatsApp and Facebook Messenger are starting to replace emails, the unstructured nature of message platforms can make it difficult to follow. A task manager guides you to fill out important sections and sorts the information for you. It's also useful in training new staff members as everything is in one place.

Even if you have a client who wants to use email, using a task manager at your end is still an option because any tasks you assign to them will be sent to their inbox and they can reply from there. In a sense, it's the best of both worlds.

> **PRO TIP:** I recommend that you turn off notifications from those email/task manager crossovers, so you don't double up.

There are many different task managers to choose from.

i.ii. Recommended platform

Based on what I have outlined above, I recommend Asana[1]. I really like the user interface. I have trained hundreds of clients and VAs to use Asana, and they pick it up quickly. It is very intuitive, and it has a great mobile app. The other advantage is the cost. Most of our community use the free version. There is a premium version which allows you to create templates. We do have some workarounds, though, for this.

I like companies which specialise in only one thing. They have all their revenue relying on this product so they spend 100% of their time looking to improve it so they can continue as a market leader. The founders are ex-Google, and ex-Facebook senior executives and have a tremendous mission — to help humanity thrive by enabling all teams to work together effortlessly. Check it out on YouTube: https://www.youtube.com/user/AsanaTeam

If you would like to find out how you can get Asana set up with everything you need in one session, go to this link: https://bookme.name/paulhiggins/mentoring

ii. Video conferencing

In my opinion, there's a lot of time wasted in meeting someone face-to-face. Video conferencing allows you to be anywhere in the world to do your work. The whole reason you left working for someone is to be able to have freedom, and video conferencing gives you this.

Video conferencing also allows you to tap into people who were hard to access previously. As you become a global citizen, you'll be able to get access to the best experts, no matter where they live.

1   https://app.asana.com/

ii.i. Recommended platform

We recommend Zoom[1]. The three things I like about Zoom are the price, the security and the user interface.

Zoom has a free account which gives you 100% functionality for 40 minutes. It allows you to test the platform and, if you like it, you can then sign to a plan. The time saved in travelling and sales calls will more than pay for itself.

Many people use Skype. I personally found there was too much spam. I have no experience with Skype for Business.

Finally, Zoom's user interface is very appealing. It is easy to use and has a great mobile app.

iii. Calendar scheduling tools

A calendar scheduling tool is a simple way of someone picking an available time in your diary without playing email ping-pong.

It works especially well when there are different time zones involved as it will automatically calculate the time in your home city. Most people will delegate that sort of task to their VA, but your VA could be doing other, more effective tasks.

When you provide a link, the tool allows someone to access a page that's linked to your calendar, and to choose a meeting slot from the free time available in your diary. You can tailor the parameters to suit you.

---

1   https://www.zoom.us/

iii.i. Recommended platform

We recommend Book Like a Boss[2]. What I like about Book Like a Boss is the user interface, continual improvement and its lite version.

There are some great options out there like Calendly[3], Acuity[4] and ScheduleOnce[5]. Personally, I like the user interface of Book Like a Boss. It looks modern and is very easy to customise. It seems like every month, there are new updates. They seek feedback from users and make tweaks to improve the platform.

Finally, there is a lite version where you can give out a link without having to have the full information page. This is useful if you are using the booking links with internal people or people who know you well. Who wants to read all about you again?

iv. Sales customer relationship management

A sales customer relationship management (CRM) tool is a database of your contacts and a template of how you go through the sales process with a prospective client. There are email distribution tools — such as Keap, ActiveCampaign, MailChimp, Ontraport, Drip, etc. — which you can use when you're sending out emails to people. However, I classify these as marketing automation tools. Some people love having it all in one. Having done both, I prefer to separate them. This is a personal preference — like choosing a Mac or PC.

Most sales are still carried out over email or phone call. It can get confusing to keep track of follow-up. Sometimes you'll have a client where you've had a conversation and they're ready to buy but life gets busy, you miss it and

---

2   https://partners.booklikeaboss.com/709.html
3   https://calendly.com
4   https://acuityscheduling.com
5   https://www.oncehub.com/scheduleonce

you don't follow up. It is common for people only to follow up once, but it's a game of constantly connecting to these potential clients because other people can get very busy too. They might intend to buy, but they've just got other things going on as well. We recommend 7-9 follow-ups. Avoid using the word follow-up. Be creative and use appropriate humour. Change each message.

A sales CRM makes following up easier. You have all the contact information in one place, so you can refresh your memory on how you met them and any personal information you've got about them. It's like having a little black book in a way — but digital. Also, it will tell you how many days since you contacted them and the total contacts.

It also allows you to delegate parts of the sales process to your VA. This can direct 30-50% of your time to more client-facing sales calls.

Having spent 26 years using sales CRMs, I could write a book on the topic. At Coca-Cola, I was on a global project looking at different sales CRMs within the company and other blue chips. Coca-Cola alone had 152 different CRMs. I am also the co-founder of a tech consulting business called Scale My Empire http://www.scalemyempire.com.

If you would like specific help, email me at paul@buildlivegive.com.

iv.i. Recommended platform

I will split my recommendations here to cover two different email platforms. Gmail and Outlook.

The sales CRM I recommend for Gmail is Copper[1]. You can easily check if someone's read an email that you sent them, the time they read it and the number of times they viewed it. You can use that information to figure out whether it's time to connect with them or not, and you can also see when you last contacted them and took them through the sequence. Other team members can also view it. Instead of having a whole lot of

---

1   https://buildlivegive.com/Copper

tasks or a whole lot of emails buried, you can allocate blocks of time to focus on sales and see where all of your prospects are within a particular sales pipeline.

The other major benefit is scraping data from the web to auto-populate fields. This can include their website, email, social media profiles and any other useful information. This can save you or your VA valuable time. It all happens in your inbox.

For Outlook, I recommend HubSpot[2]. The free version has fewer features than Copper, however, the user interface is very good.

The paid version of HubSpot has similar features to Copper. There is a 5-license minimum.

v. Password managers

I'm sure that you've seen lots of posts warning you about using a single password for everything. In today's world, white-collar crime is becoming more and more prevalent — lots of scams, people getting hacked, lots of identity theft. People will often use their children's names, their own name and family birth dates within their passwords because it's easy to remember. But this leaves you vulnerable.

A password manager limits this vulnerability. By using a password manager, you can quickly access a website using thumb and face recognition. You can also allow other people to access your sites without seeing your password. You then have the controls to remove them with a few clicks.

---

2   https://www.hubspot.com

v.i. Recommended platform

We recommend Lastpass[1] for its affordability, user interface and reputation with the outsourcing world.

Lastpass has a free account, and then the paid account is approximately USD$2 per user per month for an individual account, at the time of writing this book. This is very affordable. The paid account allows for sharing across multiple devices. The user interface is my personal favourite. If you use Google Chrome as your browser, there is also an extension available.

vi. Personal knowledge capture

When at FranklinCovey, we delved deep into neuroscience. It was fascinating to understand how the brain works. Even though we use it every second, few people understand their brain and how best to leverage it at work. As a society, every two days we create as much information as we did from the dawn of civilization up until 2003, according to Eric Schmidt ex-CEO of Google. The greatest learning is to avoid overload.

The constant bombardment of information can be draining. The analogy I use is going to a children's party and your children are scattering their belongings everywhere. One approach is to remember to grab it all as you leave. Risky! Another option is to collect their belongings as you see them and put them with your car keys. You need your car keys to leave the party, so you're not relying on your memory to collect everything at the end as you are saying farewell.

It's getting more and more difficult to remember everything. Most people can't remember people's phone numbers due to speed dial.

Albert Einstein said, 'The smartest person in the world is not one that knows all the knowledge, he just knows where to get it.'

---

1   https://www.lastpass.com/

I believe in having a virtual memory. Each time I collect a piece of information, I put it into an electronic notetaker and tag it in a couple of different ways so I can access it quickly when I need it. This has become particularly important when it comes to my health.

The health system is notorious for asking you for the same information over and over again. I have kept every conversation and important details, so I am in control of my health.

Here's a quick story to illustrate the importance of your virtual memory. I had taken a note about not having a blood transfusion as it could potentially impact the matching of my kidney donor and therefore make the transplant unlikely. This would mean another six years on dialysis.

Post my nephrectomy (kidney removal) my hemoglobin count was low, and a consulting doctor said I was to get a transfusion. I said no, and the doctor didn't want to take my word for it. I showed him my notes, he ate humble pie, and I now have a brilliant kidney from my best mate.

In business, I collect facts and tag them so they can be retrieved to answer questions for our community. This lessens the fear of forgetting something, which creates stress and anxiety. Most importantly, I can get a quick answer for a member.

If you like to write down notes physically , that is understandable. I do, as well. There are two options. One is to take a photo and then add it to the digital notebook and tag it. The software is smart enough to read the handwriting, so you get the best of both worlds. The second is to use something like Rocketbook[2]. You write with a pen which can be erased with water. You take a scan on the mobile phone app, and it will send it to a digital location of your choice.

In a sales proposal, you can put the exact words used by your prospect client in the proposal.

---

2   http://www.getrocketbook.com/

PRO TIP: Use shortcuts in your digital notebook to access regularly used information quickly.

vi.i. Recommended platform

Based on what I have said above, I recommend Evernote[1]. Evernote is platform-agnostic, easy to use and cost-effective. There is a lot of talk about Notion[2], but I like to keep tasks and notes separate. Personal choice.

Many notetaking platforms are linked to their own platform e.g. Google keep, Onenote and Apple notes. This is changing; however, I prefer to be independent.

The user interface of Evernote is very easy to use.

Finally, Evernote costs USD$7.99 per month for premium at the time of writing this book. This allows you to sync across multiple devices. Doing away with paper and pens alone will more than save you the monthly subscription!

vii. Messenger apps

Text messages have been what people respond quickest to from my experience. While it's fantastic in the past, the feature set is now lacking. Personally, I want to be able to archive my text messages — to name one gap.

Communicating via email also opens you up to the addictive trap of getting lost in your inbox, as mentioned in Chapter 4. I get my VA to triage my emails. Chat messenger is purely for immediate questions.

---

1   https://www.evernote.com/
2   https://www.notion.so/

The key here is to pick the one that you love and stick to it. Of course, there'll always be some clients who prefer others, and that's okay. But you want to pick what the majority of your clients are using. Some examples are Facebook Messenger, WhatsApp, Chatter, Slack, Yamma and Voxer. So there are quite a few options out there.

vii.i Recommended platform

We love Voxer[3]. It is like a walkie-talkie. When you start to send a voice message, the recipient instantly receives it, so the delay is minimal. You can see if someone's read (listened to) your message. The full feature set is far greater than SMS.

viii. Browser extensions

A browser is just the window you use to get information through the internet. Three of the most popular are Safari, Firefox and Google Chrome. Most of our clients use Google Chrome, and there are some great extensions that you can use to increase your effectiveness.

We use up to 30 — too many to list here. If you would like to find out more, view our spreadsheet here: https://buildlivegive.com/book-resources

---

3   https://www.voxer.com/

Summary

The goal of this chapter is to help you increase your personal effectiveness to give you time to focus on the other four Rapid Growth Drivers.

We covered three areas:

1. You
2. Us
3. Personal systems

There are a series of suggestions given in each section to help you to take action.

Under YOU:

▶ Sharpen up on the five energy drivers of Eat, Move, Sleep, Relax and Connect — take the lowest level driver and implement one daily habit

▶ Mindfulness — experiment with meditation

▶ Daily habits — build your successful daily habits and research an app which helps to embed it. It is estimated to take 66 days!

▶ Time blocking — without time blocking, you would not be reading this book at all. Test it yourself.

Under US:

▶ Personality profiling — pick one and test it on yourself and the team

▶ Virtual assistant — read the next chapter and take action

▶ Experts — get help from trusted experts

▶ Routines — set up your WIP and huddles

Under PERSONAL SYSTEMS:

Cover the gaps in your current systems across:

▸ Task managers
▸ Video conferencing
▸ Calendar scheduling
▸ Sales CRM
▸ Password managers
▸ Personal knowledge capture
▸ Messenger apps
▸ Browser extensions

Chapter 4
Your Virtual Assistant

Why do I need an assistant?

As discussed briefly in Chapter 3, I see a Virtual Assistant (VA) as an essential element of running your own business.

An assistant is someone that helps you with the administrative side of your role. Before computers, when the mail came in a secretary or executive assistant would open your mail and sort it, then bring you what was most important. They would also manage your meetings and all the administrative activities in your office. They would mainly work for senior executives and highly successful people. These people knew the value of time, so they made sure that someone helped them to use it better. As a result, they made better decisions, which led to making more money — a compound effect.

The technology was meant to remove the need for an assistant completely. Having a computer meant you could self-help. While this is correct to some degree, the need for a great assistant didn't disappear. When working at Coca-Cola, I had an assistant in most of my roles, and it worked very well, to the point where I would refuse to take a new role unless I had an assistant. It allowed me to spend more time on the things that only I could do.

When starting out on my own, I went to a local VA first

When I first went out on my own, I did everything myself. I was learning new things, and it was exciting. But soon I realised that it was not in my best interest to do it all, so I looked for a solution. I hired someone locally for about AUD $50 an hour. They worked for multiple business owners, so

I had them working for me for 10 hours per week. This allowed me to focus on selling and delivering (that was the theory!).

It worked well, but I wasn't making enough money to justify the high rate per hour, so I looked for another option. My business coach introduced me to the idea of a VA from the Philippines. I could hire someone full-time for the price of 10 hours with a local VA.

Why outsource to the Philippines?

The cost of living is lower in the Philippines, so VAs are fairly remunerated, and many get to work from home to look after their families and avoid the horrendous traffic. People working in the capital city of Manila can travel for two to three hours a day each way to work. In the wet season, it's even longer. The other advantage of the Philippines is the availability of good candidates. The Philippines have invested heavily in education and with 120+ million people, it provides a great candidate pool. They are also the fourth-largest English-speaking country in the world and have a great customer service ethic. Many VAs become the prime breadwinner in the house, as their parents have sacrificed to put them through university. This often leads to a high dependency on the role, which equates to loyalty and hard work.

We have connections for VAs in other parts of the world; however, the Philippines still gets the lion's share of our business.

How do I find a VA?

i. Direct

If you want to go the direct route, you will be dealing solely with the VA. You can post on job boards like Onlinejobsph[1], or you can hire through a referral. I would not recommend this if it is your first time as you may have to train them yourself, which is a big task. Also, there is a higher risk involved when you do not have the security of a mediator who can guarantee another VA to replace the outgoing VA quickly. VAs can sometimes disappear due to personal circumstances. Family and extended families can be complicated, and they take precedence over you. I had this happen to me a couple of times — not fun!

ii. Platform

There are many job platforms where you can post a job and view applications to complete the work. Some examples are Upwork and Freeeup. This way, you can make a pool of the best candidates. These VAs are freelancers and work for multiple people. The reality is that they often find it hard to manage capacity, and they will do the work for the highest paid job. High risk. Best used for specific skills or one-off projects.

iii. Agency

These companies specialise in recruiting, training and managing VAs on your behalf. You pay a premium for the agency; however, it saves you time. They also can attract better candidates because their scale allows them to provide health benefits.

1   https://www.onlinejobs.ph

If you've never dealt with a VA before, I recommend the agency model. As you become more experienced, you can reduce the cost by moving to the direct option.

Having run my own VA company for five years, I have great connections into what agencies to use. Send me an email at paul@buildlivegive.com, and I am happy to listen to your needs and guide you in the right direction.

Why do I know so much about VAs in the Philippines?

As mentioned above, I ran my own VA company in the Philippines for five years and still have a team based there. I've combined my corporate experience of having an executive assistant with hands-on experience running my own VA business. I have travelled to the Philippines more than 20 times, and I have a good understanding of the people, their culture and the different options available for VAs. I probably know more than most about VAs. It is a passion of mine.

I've chosen my VA, what now?

Once you have chosen the right model, you then need to focus on bringing a VA into your business to make them hugely successful.

I tapped into my experience from working at the Coca-Cola Company, with its 800,000+ employees globally, to create an induction and onboarding system which works. Below is a summary, and if you need more help, you can book a call at www.blgmeeting.com.

i. Induction

Have a meeting on their first day where you get to know about them and their family — which is really important in the Filipino culture. Use this meeting to understand what they're looking for from you and how they like to work. Get to know the person first and then train them for the tasks they need to perform. Also talk about yourself, your family, what your business is about and your purpose. This helps them to feel like a part of the team, and you will then understand each other from the very start.

ii. Onboarding

This is a key element in getting your relationship with a VA off to a great start. If you used an agency, they should have given the VA a base level. What you will be doing is building on this solid base.

There are four steps to onboarding:
1. Checklists
2. Training
3. Daily habits
4. Development

I will cover the key points in each. We provide training for solopreneurs. Book a direct mentoring session here: https://bookme.name/paulhiggins/mentoring

Checklists

We recommend you have checklists for consistency in onboarding. Some of the areas covered include:
- HR policies
- Infrastructure

- Personality profiling
- Basic software & Tools
- Software introductions
- Core competency training
- Job description
- Repeating tasks
- Questions in training
- Links to training videos

We have these checklists in Asana[1] to make it easy to implement and add learnings as you bring in new people.

Training

What you put into training in the first month will pay you back over time. I know you are busy and have many things to do. Training a VA seems like you are falling further behind, and you thought a VA was meant to take tasks from you. Solid training is a short-term sacrifice for long-term payback. I recommend you block a minimum of an hour a day for training during the first week and then 30 minutes a day for the first fortnight. I have a team of people who help with the training. If you have the same, you can move quicker.

First, it is really important to understand the learning style of your new VA. We use a free tool called VARK[2] to see what their learning style is so we can adapt our approach.

I had a recent VA who was slow on picking up tasks. In hindsight, we had skipped doing this step. When her results came back, she was a 90% visual learner. I had been giving her tasks through Voxer — in audio. I changed to screen recording what I wanted her to do, and her performance improved.

1   https://asana.com
2   http://vark-learn.com/

Combine this with the learning from the personality tests. Tony Robbins provides a free profiling tool called DISC[1]. It helps you to understand their personality and natural preferences. Ask them to give you insight into what they learnt from the tool and how it will apply to the role. Another personality profiling tool is Personality Assessor[2]. The free version gives you the big five model.

Review the last training session at the start of the next training session. As an owner, you want to move as much work to your new VA as quickly as possible, so that you can focus on what only you can do. I get it. Culturally, many Filipinos will say yes, first. They'll say they understand it to please you and avoid confrontation.

At the start of each session, ask the VA to train you on what was learnt from the last session. You will quickly realise the parts which they said they understood and should have said they didn't understand. Go back and correct this before you add more to their plate. Again, this can be frustrating but valuable in the long term.

Linked to this is the way you train. I call it the I/WE/YOU method. I learned this from a mentor of mine, James Schramko.

I = You do the task first. It's a good idea to screen record it.

WE = You and the VA both do it together. Let them take the lead, and you can fill in the gaps. Be supportive and give them confidence.

YOU = They train you on what they just learned.

Training needs to be ongoing. I will cover this in the development section in a moment.

If you need help with training, learn more at www.blgmeeting.com

---

1   https://www.tonyrobbins.com/disc
2   https://www.personalityassessor.com/bigfive/

Daily habits

The easier you make the role, the greater the chance of success. Obvious, I know, but I see so many examples of the obvious not being implemented.

The way to help make it easier is to establish daily habits for the VA to follow. They can be set up in three ways:

1. Playbooks
2. Standard operating procedures
3. Repeating tasks

Let me explain each quickly.

A playbook is often referred to in American football or the National Football League. It is a set of plays which are learned and executed with precision when a combination of elements come together. The team doesn't have to make it up on the spot — they have trained for it and know exactly what to do.

This principle can apply to your business. The playbook is continually added to when a new situation is encountered.

Standard operating procedures (covered in more detail in Chapter 8 on high-performing teams) are the details which sit behind the playbook. They are what you would refer to in training — a step-by-step guide to doing something which is core to the operational running of the business.

The next level is embedding repeating tasks in your project/task management system so that the VA doesn't have to remember the trigger to start the sequence of tasks needed to achieve the goal. As mentioned previously, we use Asana[3]. A new VA is often overwhelmed by learning the processes, so we take away much of this stress by asking them to go to their task list in Asana, which will have what they need to do for the day. This gives them certainty and structure. It also gives you visibility as to what they are doing, and if they are coping well or drowning. If you would like to see how we do this in real life, just go to www.blgmeeting.com

---

3   https://asana.com

Some other tips on habits:

- Have no more than ten outstanding tasks and ten current tasks in a task manager at any time — ask your VA to prioritise and change dates to achieve this

- Use voice to task — send your VA an audio message using something like Voxer[1]. If immediate, they do the task and archive it. If it is more involved, then they put it into their task manager, and you get notified on completion.

- End of day report — they send you a quick update with their biggest win, top achievements for the day, what they need help with. You can also track their capacity using traffic light colours — red, amber or green. Green is good, amber you need not to delegate as much work and red, best to have a meeting to resolve it.

Development

As mentioned, start with training and then follow on with continuous development. What you put in, you get back. I see some business owners fall into the trap of killing the golden goose. They keep overloading their VA and begin expecting them to do tasks they are not trained to do. The VAs either burn out or lose confidence, which impacts motivation, engagement and performance.

If you worked for a company in your past which developed you well, apply these principles to your VA. Coca-Cola believed in development and had some of the world's best practice in this space. I have adapted this to develop VAs. If this is not a strength of yours, reach out to someone who can help you to help them. Alternatively, email me at paul@buildlivegive.com, and I can help or point you in the right direction.

Some elements to consider for development:

- Immediate feedback: When your VA does something well or shows areas which need improvement, give them immediate feedback. In Australia, we play Australian football (AFL), and they talk about

1   https://www.voxer.com/

going the ball and not the player. Same with feedback — don't make it personal. Talk about the competency shown and the impact of getting it right or wrong. I ask my VAs to document it in their own words in a Google Doc, and we review it in their personal review — typically trimesterly.

▶ Above and below the line: When developing your VA, consider what you can do (above the line) and what they can do (below the line). Some solopreneurs only look at below the line. It is often the owner who needs to adapt to make the development more effective for the VA

▶ Great VAs are sought after and can often get more money working for someone else. The reason they will stay with you is largely due to the development they get. Curious people love to learn. I continually develop my VAs and, in turn, get some less experienced VAs to remove some of the lower-level tasks. This leverages their strengths, pushing them into areas they didn't think were within them.

iii. What can a VA do for me?

I could write a whole book on this topic. In this questionnaire https://buildlivegive.typeform.com/to/faCKLx, we give you a list of the common tasks a VA can do for you.

Some popular examples are:
1. Sales follow-up
2. Posting to social media
3. Monitoring social media
4. Triage your incoming messages

A simple exercise I ask the Build Live Give community members to do prior to preparing for a VA is taking note of all the tasks you do for a week and allocating them to one of three columns;

1. Delete
2. Delegate
3. Do

This can be done in a Google Sheet or using tags in your project/task management platform. The delegate column is what goes to your VA.

One item to be aware of is believing your VA is superhuman — capable of everything. A general VA can do many tasks, as you saw in the questionnaire above. However, there are some tasks best done by an expert. They could include website backend, graphic design, content writing, podcast editing, video editing, etc. We have hundreds of vetted experts you can tap into. Find out more https://buildlivegive.com/more-leads

Summary

Some of you reading this might be thinking, '*I can't pay myself, let alone pay for a VA.*' Fair point. If you are experiencing this and don't have the personal funds to invest in a VA at this point, please complete the other drivers first, to find funds to pay for a VA.

The other option is to tap into your savings and back yourself. The time you save by using a VA will be used well in implementing the other drivers, and the long-term payback will be well worth it.

A part-time VA will cost USD 400-600 per month. At the high end, this is approximately USD 7 per hour. Most solopreneurs are making 10-15 times that an hour. The numbers stack up. It is often the fear of what do they do, how to let go, and if you'll get more business that holds you back.

The joy of running your own business is making brave calls and backing yourself. I see getting a VA as a low-risk option. I've never had a client regret the decision to employ a VA.

Key actions from this chapter:

▸ Decide on what geography

▸ What model to use. Direct, platform or agency.

▸ Onboard them covering Checklists, Training, Daily habits and development.

▸ Decide what you will get them to do by going through the exercise of looking at your tasks and deciding what you can Delete, Delegate and Do

Chapter 5

Rapid Growth Driver 2 — Ideal Client

This chapter, as the name suggests, is about picking your ideal client. When you start your own business, you chase revenue in order to match the income you're used to so that you can maintain your lifestyle. There is an urgency in getting new clients to generate revenue fast. I get it, and I did exactly the same thing.

What this often leads to is chasing the wrong clients and actually slowing your growth. Let me explain.

In the haste to fill up the revenue, you get lumped with work you really don't want to do or have the skills to do. This can result in poor results, which inhibits the greatest source of leads for a solopreneur — referrals and introductions.

In a survey of small business owners, they said 85% of their new customers came from word of mouth referrals[1].

Satisfied clients will refer you to others like them. If you take on the wrong type of clients and don't get them a result, the chance of referrals declines.

It also delays all the important processes like getting your marketing message right, getting the sales process right and finalising your IP. If you constantly pivot between different cohorts, you'll find it hard to test what is working so that you can double down. You get confused, and so do your prospective clients. Your greatest supporters, looking to refer new clients into your network, don't know who you are targeting.

And, most importantly, it takes longer to get great customer testimonials and case studies. What potential clients ultimately want is social proof. Without a clear ideal client profile, social proof is almost non-existent. This makes it much harder for you to attract new clients — where's the proof you can provide what they need?

By selecting your ideal client first, you do lose a bit of short-term cash flow, but it's like what Einstein says: 'He who understands it, earns it. He who doesn't, pays it.' Granted, Einstein was talking about compound interest,

---

1   https://www.entrepreneur.com/article/302229

but the same theory applies here. Once you get it right, it compounds very quickly. You should go slowly at the start and then build momentum, as opposed to being like a machine gun and firing all the time randomly.

We live in a world where technology provides the opportunity to serve clients no matter where you are located. Solopreneurs can work and service clients from anywhere in the world. In the old days, clients would have typically said, 'I need a specialist that lives in this area,' so, therefore, service providers tended to be jacks-of-all-trades because of their location limitations. Now it's flipped the other way. You need to be very clear on what you do and specialise in. With the advances in technology, location is no longer an inhibitor to growth.

The riches are in the niches

It's that classic case of being a small fish in a large sea or the largest fish in a very small pond. I prefer being the largest fish. Instead of saying 'I do this, I do that, and I do that,' having a special focus can make you stand out to your prospective clients. It's like when you go to buy a car at a multi-brand dealership. The salesmen who are jacks-of-all-trades might not be specialists in the particular car you're looking for. You can't be sure that you got the best advice for your specific situation.

The easiest way to find a niche is to create a hierarchy of skills. What are your unique abilities? What are you excellent/good/okay at? I went through this journey myself, and I lost so much time trying to be all things to all people. But this won't help our ideal clients. A confused buyer never buys. Instead, by getting specific, we are able to provide clients with our expertise to get them a result. Ultimately this is the most important point. These days, clients care less about your skills, abilities and background — they only truly care about their self-interest and getting a result.

It's the same thing when pursuing new clients. It's much better to be specific on who the ideal client is and then work from there. The template later in this chapter will go into multiple levels to find out exactly who the ideal client is and what their pain points are.

As an example, at Build Live Give, we don't serve people who are raising funding to go global. I am a strong believer in mentoring people based on my past experience. I have not raised an angel round or Series A. I have invested in angel rounds, but this is not the same. So I am very clear and quick to refer someone who does this as part of their niche. Our ideal client is looking to use their business to fund their lifestyle and give back. I am not saying one is better than the other. What I am saying is, there is a choice.

Our ideal clients are funding their growth from working capital (cash earned from happy clients). Hypergrowth where you lose money for seven or eight years before making a profit is not the model we support. Solopreneurs need to draw out cash as they grow because the likelihood of a sale, exit or IPO is very remote.

Being clear about who we serve makes it easy for the prospective client to make a decision about whether to do business with us.

I don't have a specific quote on saying no to clients. However, if you are not saying no to 50% of inbound leads because they don't meet your ideal client criteria, this is typically a sign that there's work to be done on defining the ideal client.

Now, I can hear people saying, 'But I'm going to miss out on a lot of opportunities.' This is true, but quality over quantity is typically a smarter longer-term play. This book is helping solopreneurs to build a million-dollar annual turnover business which funds their lifestyle. All people need is a thousand raving fans paying a $1,000 per year to hit the number.

Why is choosing your niche important?

i. Meet Scott

Scott, Co-founder of Scale My Empire http://www.scalemyempire.com, is incredibly knowledgeable about scaling service-based businesses with 20-30 employees through leveraging people, processes and platforms.

But when he left the safety of the resource industry to start his own business, he tried many different directions to get traction. While it all related to generating more operational efficiency, leading to greater cash flow, the cohorts he tested were many and varying. He tried lawyers, accountants, financial planners, small business owners, digital agencies, tradies etc... etc I will stop there. You get the picture. As Scott reads this, I can see him blushing.

He was trying to hit a bullseye, but he was targeting the whole dartboard. And, in some cases, several dartboards at once.

It was difficult for him to keep the momentum going and test messages because he changed direction constantly. He also learned that, in some industries, the pain point and the problems that he was solving weren't a priority.

I like the analogy of a severe problem as your hair on fire. If a potential client has a 'hair on fire' problem, they must get it solved — and fast. If Scott was confused, imagine how a potential client felt when they visited his website.

He would spend about three months trying to contact people within a specific industry, getting sales scripts right and learning about the industry. Then he'd realise that it wasn't right, so he had to pull back and start again. For example, financial planners have a lot of regulations and a lot of red tapes, so they find it hard to scale their business. Once he learned this, he stopped trying to break into that industry.

I do believe in testing and pivoting. But tackling many fronts at once weakens your defences.

And he had another big problem — he was paying himself to sell, but he wasn't converting any sales, and he was running out of cash. He ended up having to find a financial backer willing to loan him the capital to keep afloat.

Imagine the pressure this put on Scott and his wife. They were looking to purchase a house and start a family. Scott knew something needed to change — and fast.

So Scott looked for patterns in past clients to see where best to focus. He also looked at some of the most successful software as a service (SAAS) — a method of software delivery and licensing in which software is accessed online via a subscription, rather than bought and installed on individual computers — products and where they had success. Finally, he looked at his strengths and experience — what he was good at and what he liked to do.

This all led to one area in particular — digital agencies. Once he picked this, he then went into research mode to validate his hypothesis of how to get results for them.

He interviewed past clients, industry influencers and existing experts servicing this market. He used our ideal client template to structure his questions.

The side benefit was sales calls and introductions gained by taking a diagnostic approach rather than a prescriptive approach. This relieved the pressure off Scott to sell and also refined his methodology to get better results.

Fast forward to today, and Scott targets independently owned digital agencies (predominantly paid advertising) which have 20+ staff, high demand for their services and are struggling to match their team's capability to complete the work in a profitable way.

Since defining his ideal client, Scott has been able to increase his cash flow and his revenue and is on the way to owning that dream house.

When he goes on a podcast or is speaking, he is very clear on who he serves and has some great case studies to prove it. The number of happy client referrals and introductions has increased, and his use of LinkedIn sales navigator to find his ideal client is working exceptionally well.

Now, many of you reading this may be struggling with the concept of niching down and saying no to clients who are willing to pay you money right now to fix a problem. I hear you, and it is a common fear when narrowing down on your ideal client.

The simple example I use is Coca-Cola. They had a core target consumer for all their marketing and advertising, but the product was consumed by a broader audience. When someone outside of your ideal client profile approaches you, and you can use all of your existing methodologies to get them a result then, sure, help them. It is never completely black and white, and you will always have exceptions. But it is just that — an exception and not the norm. Your marketing message is clear and creates certainty in the mind of the buyer.

ii. Meet Meryl

Meryl, the Founder of Bean Ninjas, is in a very crowded space — bookkeeping. Previously, she worked in accounting and consulting, with most of her clients in a similar geographical location to her. But to scale beyond herself, she wanted to productise her business and expand globally.

To not get lost in the pack, she wanted to create a point of difference and be clear on who her ideal client was.

Like most solopreneurs, this is not a set-and-forget strategy. Meryl had several pivots before she narrowed down to her ideal client was and what platforms she would help them with.

The word strategy, to me, means the art of making choices. Some people make choices quickly and focus. Others take time and let the market define it. Neither is right or wrong — just different approaches to getting to the ultimate decision.

Meryl ended up deciding to target lifestyle entrepreneurs using the Xero[1] accounting platform. All her clients have fewer than 200 staff, which married well with the Xero's ideal client. But she has a specific vertical focus by choosing to work with entrepreneurs. Most of her clients work within the spaces of e-commerce, business coaching and consulting. Her niche allows her to confidently get on a sales call, knowing she has very clear examples of what her service provides and what results clients can expect.

By identifying her niche and keeping her business model clear, she has attracted an investor to continue to grow her share of her home market Australia, while expanding into the U.S. and Europe.

The benefit of clearly defining your ideal client is one-to-many sales. What do I mean by this?

A one-to-many sale is where you are selling to one person who can then promote your services to many. One of the best examples of this is communities. As an example, Build Live Give runs a community for solopreneurs who are typically running a lifestyle business. This is a great fit for Meryl. I can send out an email to my list, do a webinar or have her on my podcast to promote the value she can bring to our community. It becomes a three-way win:

> ▶ The client: They get a great bookkeeping service and know how much money they have to invest in future growth while freeing up resources to work on other activities to drive the business

> ▶ The community owner: They improve the chances of getting a result for their community member, which is their first priority. Then this allows them to attract more clients by leveraging the case study

> ▶ The expert: They get a trusted source of leads who are educated and well-vetted. This helps to keep the cost of sales and marketing

---

1   https://www.xero.com

lower, to invest back into improving their product/service whilst taking out cash to fund their lifestyle.

The ideal client template: building a profile

As mentioned above, at Build Live Give, we use a template to answer the most important questions. I will give you the high-level topics here and a link to get the template:

- Details of the person
- Description
- A business they own or work in (could be multiple)
- Fears, frustrations, needs and aspirations
- What keeps them awake at night
- What type of comments they say often, and the common language they use
- Their critical success factors
- Who they follow — this could include thought leaders and experts
- What content they consume
- What communities they belong to
- Who they trust
- Who they see before and after you
- What keyword search terms they use

Often, you're so in love with your product that you will lead with the features of your product rather than understanding what is most important to the prospective client and what success looks like for them. I find this more evident in larger and more established companies. The pressure to meet market expectations and short-term results can make it harder not to be biased by what is in it for you rather than what is in it for the client. I work with many solopreneurs and often this mindset shift is necessary, but hard to do.

By going through these questions, it gives structure to solve this inward-looking philosophy.

You get to understand their pain points and put them first. It will cover how your ideal client finds you, what their specific pain point is, and what keyword searches will lead them to you (you can use companies like SEMrush[1] and KWFinder[2] for keyword searches).

If you're a little hesitant about selling, don't be. A lot of people are scared of selling. I hear comments like, 'I just don't want to sell. I'll avoid it like the plague.' Instead of calling it sales, call it research. What you're doing is researching to find out where someone is, where they want to be, what things are in their way, and if you can best help them solve their problems and get them a result. We will cover more of this in Chapter 7, about sales focus.

When writing a blog or updating website copy or your social media profiles and posts, use the exact language collected from the ideal client profile work to connect with them. Ideally, if the potential client can be subconsciously saying, 'This is exactly me,' when they read it, the chances of helping them are far greater.

Another question I often get asked is, 'How many profiles should I have?'

I recommend having two, to begin with.

One is your ideal client. It is the most likely one from a possible selection of several. You are having more than one can get confusing.

The other is your ideal partner. As mentioned above, the one-to-many sale to a community or a joint venture partner can help you scale fast whilst

---

1   https://www.semrush.com/
2   https://kwfinder.com/

keeping the cost of new client acquisition down. I will talk more about joint venture partners in Chapter 7.

i. But is this profile useful in the real world?

John Lee Dumas runs a very successful podcast called *Entrepreneur on Fire*[3], and he talks about the one individual (avatar) that he based his whole show and marketing on. That profile was actually a reflection of him as an individual and embodied what he was looking for to launch his entrepreneurial career.

He then went out and researched to make sure that the profile of his audience was right. He's definitely seen the power of being very specific around who his ideal client is.

Here is a link to a blog quote on the topic: https://www.eofire.com/defining-your-avatar/

ii. Why is this information so important?

Many people have approached me, confused about why they haven't been able to achieve their revenue targets. After walking them through this template, they've clarified their vision of their ideal client and applied it to their website, their marketing copy and their referrals. And they've gotten results from putting the hard work in.

Many people believe they know all this information — that they know their clients back to front. But once they start answering the questions in the ideal client template, they realise they actually don't know the clients as well as they should.

Once you've answered the questions, you can make a routine to go back and fill out based on more research into your clients. We set this up as a repeating task. It is always evolving.

---

3   https://www.eofire.com

iii. Interviews

So you've got your ideal client hypothesis. Now you need to go and interview people who meet your ideal client profile. This will help you validate the assumptions you've made or fill in the gaps in information. You can go back to your best clients and interview them, but it's best to do it to new or potential clients as their judgement isn't clouded by your previous performance. What you're doing in this process is understanding exactly what they want and then coming up with your product. This is much easier than coming up with a product and then trying to find an audience to sell it to.

Ask why people are doing what they do and why they need your services. Most people think it's about money. They assume people want to make more money. But often it's actually not about that. That's just the first level. What they are going to do with that money — that is the real question! They might have an overseas trip they want to go on; they might want to renovate their house. They might want to give their daughter or son a car or pay for their wedding. There are certain things that money provides them, and you need to get to that — because it's the result that's important, not the feature. People will still buy on emotion. They won't buy on fact.

As an example, after filling out this template, Scott did some interviews. He talked to owners of digital agencies, and their answers were things he didn't expect. He thought it was all about money, but he realised it just funded what they really wanted. In some cases this was school fees, overseas holidays, putting in a pool, supporting ageing parents, etc. He shifted from a fact-based sale to an emotion-based sale, which resonated strongly with his ideal clients as the old saying goes.

'People buy on emotion and validate on facts'.

I experienced this for myself. I assumed that because I left corporate, everyone would make decisions the same way. I was so emotionally invested in the product that I thought that everyone thought like me. When I stepped back and did this exercise, I realised my reason for running my own business was not the same as others. Sounds obvious, but I was so passionate and focused on the delivery value that I forgot to ask some simple, yet powerful questions.

iii.i. How do I get started?

Because it's not sales, it's actually researching; these interviews are quite enjoyable. It's best to begin within a network where there is trust. Within your LinkedIn community, you should have enough people. I've found most solopreneurs are willing to invest half time to help. You are always looking to add value back. If there are problems, you can solve, do it as a thank you for their commitment to you.

Some people get nervous when interviewing, and I understand. The best way to overcome this is to practise. Start with a family member, practise it, and iron out the kinks. Then research someone within a direct network to build up to unknown people who are referrals.

Everyone can interview. The common fear of rejection is soon overcome. The hardest element is to pick one ideal client.

There's a couple of ways to do the interviews. One is to do interviews over the phone or video conference. The other is to send a form for them to fill in and return. I recommend doing a combination of both.

Please don't make these common excuses for not doing interviews:

▶ 'Yeah, look, I'm too busy, I just need sales.'

▶ 'I haven't got time to do this.'

▶ 'Clients are too busy, and they don't have time to talk to me.'

Be aware of the tendency to move the interview into a sales call. The interviewee may encourage it, but I highly recommend setting up a separate sales call.

If you have a social group — like a Facebook group — this is a great way to listen in and test what your ideal client is struggling with and learn how you can help them. One of the best examples of this is Jill and Josh Stanton from Screw the Nine to Five community[1]. They have a large and private Facebook community[2] and use it for research.

---

1   https://www.screwtheninetofive.com
2   https://www.facebook.com/SayNoToNinetoFive

iv. Double down and find your ideal client

After these interviews, you will have the elements you need to define your ideal client. Take some of these elements, plus the knowledge learnt during the conversations, to create a client rating system to match potential clients against a set of criteria.

To see our example, go to https://buildlivegive.com/book-resources

We have the bar set at 70%. If they rate above this, I will have another call with them. If it is below, I will refer them to someone else or nurture them until they are ready.

One of the great advantages of running your own business is to be very selective on who you work with. Don't give up this benefit lightly.

iv.i. So why double down?

I had a past client, Aleks, who was a member of our Build Live Give community. On his website, he said he serviced startups, business owners, and enterprise clients. One day, we sat down for a chat, and I asked him how that was going.

'It's really confusing.'

'Well, it's really confusing for me as well. When I look at your website, it's a messy variation between those three demographics.'

What made this more telling was that Aleks was a brand strategist.

He used our ideal client systems and narrowed his ideal clients to business owners with less than 200 staff. He got very specific and then launched his new website, targeted towards this ideal client. He got immediate traction.

Summary

Identifying your ideal client is crucial for success. By using the ideal client template, you will be able to know if a potential client fits into your ideal or not.

If 85% of sales come from referrals and introductions, make it easy for people to know who you serve.

Having a wide field of interviews to gather information from will help you narrow down your template to fit just your top three ideal clients. From there, choosing a specific potential client to talk to will make your marketing, sales and web copy much stronger and will help you attract the right people.

Make sure that you let go of your preconceived ideas about your ideal client, and don't be afraid to go out, do the research and talk to people. There's a time for sales, and this isn't it. Trust the process of the interviews. It has been successful many times within our Build Live Give community, and there is no reason why you can't use it too. This isn't just for small business owners. Every key brand in the world does this — we've just made it shorter and simpler for you.

Some actions from the chapter:

- Create two ideal client profile. Client and Joint Venture partner. Use the ideal client template
- Set a hypothesis and interview people to prove or disprove it
- Dig deeper to find the emotional benefits and their personal wins for working with you
- Separate a sales call from the interview
- Use social media groups to gain insights (can be your group or others). Always play by the rules of the group

▸ Set up your ideal client rating system here https://buildlivegive.com/book-resources

In the next chapter, we'll be looking at the best way to serve your ideal client by addressing their pain points and incorporating these solutions into our business model to help fund your lifestyle.

Chapter 6

Rapid Growth Driver 3 — Right Business Model

In the last chapter, we focused on getting results for the right clients. This is a critical component to running your own business. However, it should not come at the expense of achieving your goals.

When I make a financial diagnosis with new members, it normally becomes clear that they are adding value to clients at the expense of themselves.

One measure is monthly drawings — what you are paying yourself to provide value to your ideal clients.

You have probably heard the analogy of the oxygen mask on a plane. In short, you are instructed first to get your breathing sorted before you help others.

Not paying yourself often leads to complications in your private life, which spills back into your business. You live one life, and the two worlds of business and personal life are very much linked.

Often solopreneurs get trapped into creating a business model which is hugely time-intensive and reliant upon them. Your greatest strength of adding value to clients, when overplayed, becomes a noose around your neck.

The business you set up to fund your lifestyle and give back becomes a chore and begins to feel like a poorly paid job.

In this chapter, we will explore ways to balance what your client and you, the business owner, can get from the value you provide.

What is the business model?

According to Investopedia, a business model is a company's plan for making a profit[1]. It identifies the products or services the business will sell, the target market it has identified, and the expenses it anticipates.

My definition of a business model is similar; however, the elements are refined to a solopreneur's circumstances. The key elements are:

1. Non-negotiables
2. Competitors
3. Point of difference
4. Pricing

As a solopreneur, by running your own business, you have the flexibility you've always dreamt of. This flexibility can be constrained by not getting the financial results to fund the lifestyle you want.

You deliver great value for clients, but not for yourself. We will go through each of the elements to enable drawings to pay yourself and profits to reinvest in marketing and team to grow your business.

i. Non-negotiables

The non-negotiables are the starting point. Stephen R, Covey, the author of *The 7 Habits of Highly Effective People*, famously said to 'begin with the end in mind'.

A business should support your lifestyle. If not, it is best to stay working for someone else.

---

1   https://www.investopedia.com/terms/b/businessmodel.asp

Deciding on what is most important and then getting a business model to support it is a great advantage of being a solopreneur. Don't waste this opportunity.

Some examples of non-negotiables include:

- ▸ Where do I want to live?
- ▸ How many hours do I want to work?
- ▸ How much will I pay myself?
- ▸ What are the events that I want to attend each year?
- ▸ When will I take my family breaks?
- ▸ How much do I want to travel for work (avoiding nights away and planes)?
- ▸ What are my values, and what will I not compromise on?

Working for yourself provides the ability to work from anywhere in the world and at any time.

When I set out to create my business, the number one consideration was if I could run it from a hospital bed. Yes, I could have made more money by running in-person workshops and events all over the world, but with my health, it was not practical.

I am glad I did set it up this way. For three months, I sat on a dialysis machine for three days a week, four and a half hours a day. I would rather have been in a cafe overlooking a beautiful beach, but you can't always get what you want!

I was able to support my community and keep working through because I had work from the hospital as a key requirement when I planned my business model.

When mentoring people, I often come across a common complaint: they are tired and stressed by doing in-person workshops. The travel and time away from home can begin to feel like they are back to working in a job.

We work on changing their business model to transition from in-person to online. This change can be liberating.

Here is a checklist example with the key questions to answer: https://buildlivegive.com/book-resources

It is your life, and you should live it how you want.

Often I advise clients in the Build Live Give Community who have created a business which doesn't meet their life goals. If you are about to escape corporate and want to create your dream business to live the life you want, start by asking yourself these questions:

- Industry: What industry do you want to work in?
- Strengths: What are your core strengths, and how can you leverage them?
- Monthly revenue: What is the monthly revenue you need to make an income?
- Monthly income: What is the monthly income you need to draw from your business to sustain the lifestyle you deserve?
- Working hours per week: How many hours do you want to work each week?
- Big Rocks: What are the big-ticket items you want to achieve?
- Where to live: Where do you want to live?

Take time to complete this.

It is best when it works for everyone. Involve the key members of your family in this. I might use the term solopreneur, but the reality is your loved ones go through this journey with you. And if there is a business partner involved, understand their non-negotiables and align where possible.

For example, I had a coaching situation where one business partner wanted to get as much cash out of the business to fund a new house, and the other partner wanted to put it into marketing to grow their revenue. In principle, both are desirable, but the tension caused a fallout.

The best time to put this on the table is at the beginning of the relationship.

I have found that the biggest barrier to completing the checklist is one's ability to say no. People can want it all, but the people who succeed are the ones who make the hard decisions to live the life they always wanted. As Derek Sivers says: 'If you're not saying "HELL YEAH!" about something, say "no."'

The ability to say no is hardest on your own. I find the accountability of a mentor and supportive peers makes this easier. The best sports people have coaches who support them. You don't have to do it all yourself. If you would like to find out some options, please email me at paul@buildlivegive.com.

ii. Competitors

I often hear clients say, 'I never look at my competitors because I'm unique and I don't like to look in the rear vision mirror. I only look forward, creating something no one else has created before.' Or some people say, 'I've just never seen anyone else in the world like me.'

It is rare that a potential client will not have multiple options in mind when they are deciding who to work with.

The competitors don't always seem obvious to you because you are so focused on what you do. The ideal client profile, mentioned in Chapter 5, helps in identifying some of the key competitors. It's important to look at your key competitors through the eyes of the potential client at the moment they're making a decision. Walking in their shoes can only benefit both of you.

In the next chapter, I will go into my definition of what selling means. In short, you are looking from your client's perspective on each option they have in front of them and helping them to look at the pros and cons of each.

I'm constantly looking for experts to serve our members. I can typically list at least four examples of direct competitors. If there are no obvious competitors, you might want to ask yourself why. Through the use of technology, you should be able to locate someone doing what you are doing.

I like to look at competitors who are ahead of where I am. Time and testing by them can save you time. Look at their website and social media, and apply any learnings which are relevant to your business. Them make them unique to you.

When I am asking experts to support our community, some experts are coy about mentioning competitors in case I approach them as well. I believe you need to take the higher ground and be transparent. The joy of running your own business is that you don't need thousands of clients. Clients want a result and a relationship. There is only one of you in this world. If there is a blind spot, isn't it best to find it out and correct it instead of never finding out why you are missing sales?

Look at some of the heavily funded startups in the world for inspiration. They are spending huge amounts on getting the best people in the world to test and measure strategies for them. Go to their websites and learn from the best. You can then take their learning and mould it to your ideal clients.

For example, I follow Michael Stelzner, founder of Social Media Examiner[1]. He has the audience size and the resources to split-test and improve his site. I learn and adapt to my own audience.

The action from this section is to complete a competitor assessment. I would start by asking the most recent clients who else they considered before their purchase.

Then do a Google search of keywords found in your ideal client research from Chapter 5.

Once there are four to five competitors, create a Google Sheet with the company name across the horizontal axis and the following attributes down the vertical axis:

- ▸ Source of traffic
- ▸ Key marketing assets
- ▸ Website home page CTA

---

1 https://www.socialmediaexaminer.com/author/mike-stelzner

- ▸ Lead magnet
- ▸ Pricing

Their website, LinkedIn company page and key social media sites will have most of the information. You can also use SimilarWeb[1] and Lately[2] as diagnostic tools.

I recommend using your VA to do the grunt work. They can create it as a repeating task and regularly update it. Think of the tweaks made to websites and socials over the course of a year. Stay on top of the trends. Google Alerts can be set up to collect information as, well.

Defining your competitors can be hard. Take me as an example. If I was to compare all the communities helping solopreneurs, there could literally be thousands.

This is why we have you define your ideal client in Chapter 5 so that you are clear about the niche served. From my research, there are very few communities specifically targeting solopreneurs with the values Build, Live and Give.

In our sales scripts in Chapter 7, one of the questions asked is: 'Who else have you used before to solve this or who else are you considering?' This provides constant information to add to research.

iii. Point of difference

At Coca-Cola, we were trained by some of the top professors in the world (Stanford University[3] and Harvard Business School[4] in particular) on business strategy.

---

1   https://www.similarweb.com
2   https://www.trylately.com
3   https://www.stanford.edu
4   https://www.hbs.edu/Pages/default.aspx

A common theme was defining a unique value proposition (UVP). Some people refer to it as a unique selling proposition (USP). In plain English, it simply means what you do better than anybody else in the world.

Whilst I agree with the principles, I also believe a solopreneur's ability to be totally unique is a tall order. As a person, you are unique, but as a business, there could be many like companies. I prefer to go for a point of difference. It removes the heartache of trying to have something that no one else in the world has — for starters, how do you find this out anyway?

Let me give you an example. I have developed my signature system (a term I learned from Taki Moore at Million Dollar Coach[5]), which is the Five Rapid Growth Drivers. Having a signature system is not as unique as most coaches and consultants will package their knowledge this way. My point of difference is the terms I use and the way I have structured it, as explained in this book.

Another example is my membership called Build Live Give Get More Leads https://buildlivegive.com/more-leads. Having a membership is not unique. The value I am providing members is my point of difference. For example:

1. Direct mentoring — getting instant access to my 26+ years of experience
2. Experts — access to over 400 experts specifically vetted for solopreneurs
3. More leads — a proven way of generating more leads through LinkedIn

The most important point here is that you don't have to come up with something unique just for the sake of it. Getting a result for your clients is the most important reason to have a point of difference. The fact that I have a signature system and membership is not unique. The way I deliver it and get results — that is my point of difference.

If you would like some help refining your point of difference, please book a session with me www.blgmeeting.com

---

5   https://milliondollarcoach.com/

iv. Pricing

Revenue is a function of two items. There is the volume and then the price you sell it at. If I sell 1,000 ice creams and I price them at $3.50 each, I will make $3,500 in revenue. Many solopreneurs get so focused on volume, they forget about the price.

Typically there are marketing costs associated with increasing volume. This could be paid ads, copywriting, the cost of expert contractors, etc. On the other hand, increasing your prices incur fewer costs. Therefore to increase prices gradually will increase your profits more.

There are three ways of setting prices:
1. Cost-plus model.
2. Matching competitors
3. Return on investment (ROI)

Cost-plus model

This is where you take all your costs and add a margin (e.g. 40%) to arrive at your selling price. The trick here is to include all your costs.

Many solopreneurs are not great at the financials and underestimate their true cost of a sale. They may spend 12 months selling a service in which they believe they are making a gross profit, only to realise when they speak to their accountant that they were actually not charging enough.

I highly recommend getting someone to help you calculate the true cost of your service. A bookkeeper, Virtual Chief Financial Officer (VCFO) or your accountant can help. Ask me at paul@buildlivegive.com, and I can connect you with someone.

The other problem with the cost-plus model is that it may not be competitive because your cost base is too high or your competition is not aware of their cost structure, and they undercut you and the market.

Competitors

This is normally the easiest way to set your pricing. Simply look at your competitors and decide what brand positioning you want to have. Do you want to the most expensive in the market, and have higher prices and lower volume? Or do you want it to be the other way around?

At Coca-Cola, they had a saying that someone always needs to be the most expensive and it might as well be you. In the Australian market, we sold at a 20-30% premium when compared to our number one competitor. It did help to have significantly more market share to command this premium.

You will need to factor in your costs plus a margin to check if the market price is sustainable.

The trick here is to charge the market price from the start of your business. I hear many solopreneurs say they underquote because they don't have the experience of established players. Once you set your prices low, it is hard to increase them. What I recommend is charging the market rate and discounting based on tradeables. These tradeables might be linked to getting a testimonial from them, introductions to their network, recommendations on LinkedIn and a willingness to act as a referee if a future client wants to call someone.

Return on investment

This is typically the most lucrative and therefore, the hardest to do. Return on investment means calculating your pricing based off a percentage of the money the client will make from selling your product and services.

For example, the cost of service, including a margin might be $1,000. The client can make $10,000 from using the service. So the ROI for the client is 10x. In most cases, a range of 3x-6x is good.

The difficulty comes in calculating the money they will make from your service, as it can be hard to isolate — for example, providing strategic advice and specific marketing or sales which impact the result. Many coaches help to adjust the mindset of their clients. This will have an immediate and longer-term payoff, but it can be hard to qualify.

One model which can work well is a share of revenue model. A client has a run rate of $400,000 a year as a base. If it can be doubled to $800,000 in a year, the increment is $400,000. Of the increment, 10% or $40,000 goes to the solopreneur, and the client keeps 90%. This puts skin in the game for both parties. The market rate for consulting might be $2,000 a month or $24,000. Under a share of revenue model, the solopreneur is $16,000 or 66% better off.

Some quick tips to consider in revenue share deals:

- ▸ Your service directly impacts revenue — normally sales and marketing
- ▸ Have a deep assessment of clients capability to deliver — look at past success as a predictor of the future
- ▸ Have a legal agreement which spells out all scenarios — good and bad
- ▸ If the client is too eager to enter and agreement, it may not be the best fit — they are desperate
- ▸ What are the owners track record of implementing and the quality of the team around them?

I have many examples and templates. If you would like to know more, please email me at paul@buildlivegive.com.

Pricing is very important because revenue growth in a business is technically infinite. You can continue to grow it, but you can only save 100% of your costs. I learnt this saying from Don Meij, Australian Entrepreneur of the Year and owner of Domino's Pizza.

Pricing is often a mindset game and less about mathematics. It is totally normal to feel less than deserving of the prices charged.

If a problem for a client is solved and they get a significant benefit, then there is nothing wrong with charging a portion of the upside.

Content writer case study

One of our members was a content writer. Their pricing was significantly lower than the market. Their focus was on getting more customers to make up the revenue shortfall. When we did the math, they were actually losing on every client. They also had no VA. Their vital time was wasted on admin. More clients at the same price would have sent them broke.

We increased their pricing and implemented a VA. All of a sudden, they started to make a profit per job. At first, they held onto the belief they would not win any deals at the new pricing. I said, 'Test it and see. At worst, you lose the next sale. Get it right, and the upside over multiple clients can change your lifestyle.'

When you make the pricing changes, you typically 'grandfather' or retain the pricing with your old clients. You communicate this to them to thank them for their loyalty and remind them of what a great deal they have. If you gain more clients and there are some deals which are just too low, you can let them go. It is hard, but so is not having money to live the lifestyle deserved.

Best pricing structures

McDonald's spent millions of dollars in conjunction with The Coca-Cola Company on finding the best pricing structures. McDonald's have their famous small, medium and large cup sizes. Most people default to a medium. There is a fine line between offering too much choice and not enough. Three options are a good combination. Clients want to make the decision for themselves. Most SAAS companies use this model, and I highly recommend it.

Summary

The main point of this chapter is to get you to add value to your clients whilst paying yourself. We want you to work smarter, not harder.

We went through the four components:

1. Non-negotiables
2. Competitors
3. Point of difference
4. Pricing

The actions you need to take:

Non-negotiables

▸ Complete the template here https://buildlivegive.com/book-resources

▸ Get alignment with people impacted by the outcome (the people closest to you).

Competitors

▸ Ask clients who they compared you to

▸ Look at and learn from people ahead of you

▸ Look at your competitor's source of traffic, key marketing assets, website and lead magnets

Point of difference

▸ The category is not your point of difference; it is how you put your unique spin on it

▸ Create your signature system

▸ Tailor services to you

Pricing

- ▶ Cost-plus — work out the true cost of providing your service
- ▶ Matching competitors — set market price and define your tradeables
- ▶ ROI — do your due diligence for revenue share deals

In the next chapter, we cover how to market and sell your business model. So far, you've identified who your ideal clients are, and you know the right business model based on the four components in this chapter. Now what you've got to do is make sales. An offer that converts is the most important part of running your own business.

Chapter 7

Rapid Growth Driver 4 — Sales Focus

Introduction

This chapter covers both marketing and sales. Sales mean converting a client from interested in a service to paying for it. Marketing is just telling more people about what you do.

The overarching principle is finding out where someone is right now, working out where they want to be in the future and providing them with the best way to get there.

In big companies, sales and marketing are typically two completely different departments. This often leads to unnecessary confusion. The marketers say the sales teams aren't supporting the product, and the sales teams say there was not enough money spent on the marketing or that the quality of the marketing is subpar — which is code for lack of leads. Often the consumer gets forgotten about in the crossfire.

In a solopreneur's business, we need to do both. Therefore we will cover both in this chapter.

Sales are the lifeblood of any business — even more so for your own business. Getting sales right allows for cash to invest in marketing, fund a high-performing team to deliver awesome customer service and, most importantly, have the cash to fund your lifestyle and give back.

I am going to cover the three key elements of marketing:

1. Free
2. Paid
3. Joint venture

I will also mention referrals, which is a blend of free and joint ventures.

Then I'll cover the three key elements of sales:

1. Mindset
2. Skills
3. Systems

I support the views expressed in *Ready Fire Aim* by Michael Masterson[1] that solopreneurs need to do the selling to the first 1 million in sales. It is not something you can delegate or outsource to someone else, in my opinion. The good news is that it is easier to 'sell' than most people perceive. Let me show you.

Marketing

i. Getting free traffic to your business

By implementing Rapid Growth Drivers 1-3, the stage is set to attract the right clients. Most solopreneurs fund growth through clients paying them money for a product or service. It is often called working capital, which is a fancy word for cash. In the beginning, it can feel like the chicken and the egg. You don't have the cash to invest in marketing, but you need marketing to attract more clients.

I get it, and this is why I will show you the activities which have consistently worked for solopreneurs and which will give you cash fast. As you know, nothing is 'free' in the world. There is your time invested which does have an opportunity cost associated with it. The less time, the better. The overall goal is to get in front of ideal clients and build an engaged audience.

---

1   https://www.amazon.com/Ready-Fire-Aim-Zero-Million/dp/0470182024

The most common mistakes solopreneurs make, in my opinion, is to develop a service and then find clients to buy it. I am sure you have never done this, just like I haven't! A much better way is to build your audience first, using the research techniques shown in Chapter 5, and create an offer off of a need.

i.i. Podcasts

What is a podcast? Think of it as a radio station that is pre-recorded and available for you to listen to whenever you want. Podcasts were started by Apple (hence the 'pod', as in iPod). It's not a great name, but it has stuck.

Podcast outreach means getting a spot on someone else's podcast. According to Podcast Insights, at this very moment, there are estimated to be over 600,000 active podcasts. Approximately 44% of people the United States have listened to a podcast, 17% listen weekly, and up to 15% listen once per year. And of those who listen to podcasts, 80% of them will listen to a minimum of 80% of an episode[1].

What's brilliant about a podcast is that it's an 'evergreen' conversation. The content is not tied to a specific time so it can be used over and over again. It's a marketing activity with a long shelf life. It is the gift that keeps on giving.

A podcast, to me, is a conversation. If 100 people listen to the podcast, you are on; this is 100 conversations and all it took you was 30-60 minutes to create it.

Some of the larger podcasts I have appeared on, like *The Growth Experts* Podcast[2] which is hosted by the talented Dennis Brown, get thousands of downloads per episode, which boosts your reach considerably.

1   https://www.podcastinsights.com/podcast-statistics/

2   https://growthexperts.libsyn.com/e127-five-drivers-for-growing-a-7-figure-lifestyle-business-w-paul-higgins?tdest_id=1091786

Later there will be the option to launch a podcast but for now, tap into someone's existing audience which is aligned to the ideal client. Sharing knowledge and adding value will help to build the brand and audience.

Tom Schwab from Interview Valet[3] suggests you have three calls to action (McDonald's style) on a podcast in order to bring traffic to your website.

I am happy to introduce anyone to Tom. Simply email me at paul@buildlivegive.com

How to get onto other people's podcasts

First, shortlist the podcasts you want to be on. There's a couple of ways. Use Listen Notes[4] as it aggregates podcasts across multiple platforms. You can search by topic and find relevant podcasts. Or go to the individual platforms like iTunes, Stitcher, Spotify, etc. which rank the top podcasts by category. Look for podcasters who aren't a direct competitor, but who have the ideal client in their audience. Remember to add value to the audience first and drive traffic second.

With podcast outreach, many large shows (1 million+ downloads a month) are hard to direct outreach to. I use the analogy of a nightclub bouncer. To get onto the show, a VIP pass or knowing someone on the door is necessary. A podcast valet service is someone who can do this. We have several valet services we recommend, including Interview Valet, as mentioned before. To get access, simply join one of our programs. Find out more at https://buildlivegive.com/service/

For example, in Chapter 5, I mentioned John Lee Dumas, whose podcast, *Entrepreneur on Fire*[5], is one of the biggest podcasts in the world for entrepreneurs. I know Kate Erickson, who runs the business side of the show and is John's life partner. I was trying to get a friend on the show, and

3   https://interviewvalet.com
4   https://www.listennotes.com
5   https://www.eofire.com/podcast

she said, 'Sorry. We're completely booked out. We're not taking any more guests.' Then, that friend went to a valet service (via our experts), and was on the podcast within a couple of weeks. The podcast was a great source of leads for her.

The other benefit of using a valet service is they help with the pitch and preparation for the interview. This is their specialty, what they do every day. The cost of getting on the shows also covers the templates, which you can use yourself in the future. Think of it as paid education.

Developing your own podcast

Developing your own podcast is a longer-term strategy. It won't deliver immediate results, but it's a brilliant way of establishing authority and a way to create relationships at the top of your sales funnel. The definition of the sales funnel (also known as a revenue funnel or sales process) refers to the buying process that companies lead customers through when purchasing products. A sales funnel divided into several steps, which differ depending on the particular sales model.

I launched my Podcast called *Corporate Escapees* in 2017. It is now called *Build Live Give*[1].

The majority of podcasters don't get past ten published shows. It is hard work, and you can get deflated by the lack of downloads and engagement — vanity numbers. The trick is to forget the numbers and improve the quality of the content for your audience. Our *Build Live Give* podcast has had about 25,000 downloads to date. That's 25,000 conversations I've had, which I would never have had in the real world.

---

1   https://buildlivegive.com/podcast/

There are a few options in setting up a podcast.

1. Do it yourself

2. Do it with someone

3. Get it done for you

I can help you with all three. Email me at paul@buildlivegive.com.

I get people reaching out to me on LinkedIn, saying they love the podcast and would like to have a call. When we talk, it is like they know me already. The level of trust is high, and it allows me to ask better questions because I don't need to talk about myself. The less I talk, the better — leave that to the podcasting!

You can also use podcasts as a way of getting new clients. As a rough rule of thumb, 25% of your podcast guests could become clients. Our podcast interviews solopreneurs who left their job to build their own business to live and give. Their stories are inspirational and practical.

'I am a 'corporate escapee' and love Paul's podcast! I wish I had found it sooner! I escaped eight years ago and had to totally figure things out on my own. Wish I could have learned from Paul and his guests when I first started, however, my business continues to grow, and I'm finding their wisdom extremely useful as I now scale my business. Keep up the great work, Paul!'

Meg Huwar, Principal at Brand Accelerator

It is rare to have a guest decline an invite to appear on the show. Most people want to expand their audience and have valuable content to share with their existing audience. You are adding value to them first.

From a sales funnel perspective, I see three opportunities:

1. Icons

2. Brand builders

3. Bank builders

Icons

I classify an icon as a thought leader who has a significant audience and is well-respected in their industry. Some examples on my podcast are:

- ▸ James Schramko
- ▸ Nathan Chan
- ▸ Kate Erickson
- ▸ Josh Stanton

They give excellent content to your audience and also help you to get other icons on your show. They also give credibility to help get you on other podcasts.

The belief that they will share the episode to their audience is often a myth. They have their own content which they will prioritise first. I would not bank on this 'free' kick.

Brand Builders

They are people with a large community. They are more likely to share the podcast episode with their community, which helps to establish your brand. It also gives them the ability to do the same.

This collaboration is best where there are similarities in ideal clients but differences in how they are served.

Bank Builders

I know this is a little crude. This is where you interview potential clients to add value first, build a relationship and understand their key focus and what is stopping them in achieving it. If you believe you can help them, then a separate sales call is appropriate. I forecast for 25% of my bank-builder guests to be clients in some shape or form. This is above the standard sales conversion rate of 20% for a services business.

I will talk more about how to find these people in the next section.

i.ii. LinkedIn

At the time of writing this book, the social media platform LinkedIn has 500+ million active users worldwide[1]. Of that number, 250 million are active every month, and 40% are daily users. In the old days, you had a black book of contacts. LinkedIn is that but on steroids. 59% of LinkedIn companies that have less than 200 employees, so LinkedIn is a brilliant way of building service-based businesses in a B2B (business-to-business) format. It's a great way of getting new clients.

I have used LinkedIn since 2009 and consider myself knowledgeable in driving leads on the platform. I have been coached by some of the best experts on the planet and then tested their teachings and adapted it for solopreneurs.

As with all social platforms, the goalposts keep moving. What is current today will not be in the future. To stay abreast of these changes, please follow me on LinkedIn https://www.linkedin.com/in/paulhiggins555.

There are several components to LinkedIn. I will cover the key ones here and give you free training[2] to help you further. The components are:

1. Profile
2. Posting
3. Relationships
4. Sales navigator
5. Killer tips

---

1   https://www.omnicoreagency.com/LinkedIn-statistics/
2   https://buildlivegive.dubb.com/v/dUxw43

Profile

Why is your profile so important? Most people will use LinkedIn as their first point of research on a person or company. It is often viewed more than a website. My LinkedIn is viewed 10-15x more than my website.

If first impressions count, you want to make a lasting one by having a great profile. The key components are:

- ▸ A great looking profile picture
- ▸ A custom background header with an inspiring image, your brand name, who you serve and your slogan
- ▸ An impactful headline statement — what you do, e.g. mentor, podcaster, etc. Use | not emojis, to separate words. Then 'I help X to achieve Y so they can do Z.'
- ▸ Client-facing about section — not about you. Frame it to follow: pain point, agitate, solution and call to action (CTA). One CTA, email is best. Have three videos at the bottom of your About section, e.g. your story. how it works, case study
- ▸ Voluntary experience — a maximum of three
- ▸ Recommendations — have a system to ask regularly, the top two should be current
- ▸ Skills and endorsements — 40 in total, arranged in order of importance and pin your top three
- ▸ Profile views — reach out to 2nd and 3rd connections views and ask how they found you

Posts

Posts are a great way of driving eyeballs to a profile. They also give you the opportunity to send messages and start engaging with your ideal clients who like and comment on your posts. Through this, you can find out what their focus is and how you can help them to achieve it.

We have tested hundreds of scripts and have cracked the code. If you would like access to these scripts, please check out our membership at https://buildlivegive.com/more-leads

The key components are:
- Leverage the LinkedIn algorithm — this is subjective, but at the time of writing this book we believe it to be 15-20 engagements (likes or comments) in the first 30 minutes and 50 in the first hour
- Work collaboratively with other like-minded people.
- Post to 'Anyone' and to Twitter
- Repost to your favourite groups
- Your post's opening two sentences must be intriguing — act like a journalist and use this https://coschedule.com/headline-analyzer to help you write killer headlines
- Human stories work the best
- Space text in your posts as 60% of readers are viewing it on a mobile
- Use a compelling picture or video in the post
- Use hashtags and @mention people in your posts — use those with the highest followers.
- End the post with a question to encourage comments, which rank higher in the algorithm
- At the end of the post, use 8 hashtags — one signature hashtag (I use #buildlivegive) and the rest with high traffic, e.g. #sales = 5.2 million followers (feel free to follow my profile to see how I do it)
- Ask people to like the post
- Like the comments on your post and reply to them
- Direct message people who engage if they meet your ideal client template, thank them and ask what their focus is
- Minimum of three posts a week — Tuesday and Thursday are the best days to post
- Have a posting schedule with themes for every day
- Post ratio should be 60% Awareness, 30% CTA and 10% curated content

Find out more at https://buildlivegive.com/more-leads

Relationships

I used to call this section messaging, but I have learned it is about more than sending a message. It's about building a relationship. The simple analogy I use is meeting someone in a social environment — like a bar. You build rapport and the conversation flows. It has mutual respect and no cunning tricks. It usually has some humour and makes both people feel better off from the time invested. LinkedIn is a virtual version of this.

Think of the times when you receive a cold connection request with no personalised message. Then the next message you receive is a poorly worded pitch. You would delete it, right?

I see many solopreneurs with a LinkedIn process (including scripts from an expert) which mirrors this. If you would delete a message like this, why would your ideal clients behave any differently? There is a better way, and I will give you some tips here:

- ▶ Build relationships, not connections
- ▶ Treat others like you want to be treated yourself
- ▶ It is a social platform — two-way engagement
- ▶ Ask good and interesting questions which are short and encourage a response
- ▶ Add value first, e.g. liking and commenting on their recent posts
- ▶ Wait for a reply for two business days before extending a personalised invite
- ▶ Once they are a first connection, endorse their top three skills
- ▶ Look for mutual connections and ask them about how they know them
- ▶ Use humour and keep away from the general cliches, e.g. 'I see we have 178 mutual connections'

Sales Navigator

Sales navigator, for many LinkedIn users, is a mystery. It was to me, up until recently. The simplest way to describe it is like finding a needle in a haystack. You can use filters to set up a way of finding your ideal clients mentioned in Chapter 5.

This then provides the opportunity to add value to them first before reaching out using the techniques described in the relationship section above.

I use this to find my ideal clients to invite them onto my podcast.

Some tips:

▸ Set your filters up to get between 700 and 900 results

▸ Look who has engaged in the last 30 days on the platform — this increases your chances of getting a reply

▸ Like and comment on posts prior to sending connection request messages

▸ Tailor the connection request to them

Killer tips

Doing the 1%-ers helps to make a significant change. LinkedIn is like this. Small tweaks can have a material impact on results. Here are some to consider:

▸ Groups — you can send direct messages to 2nd connections

▸ If an inbound request has no personal message, send a message asking them how they found you — I ask if they have seen a post or listened to my podcast and if there's no response then I decline the message (well, my VA does)

▸ Remove any spammers from connections

▸ The first eight seconds of a video is essential — length: 30 seconds maximum, natural and with captions

- Use O-DAN for great free photos[1]
- Post without link-outs and then edit the post and add them in — this tricks the algorithm as LinkedIn doesn't like you taking people off their platform, and is better than putting the link in the comments where it can get lost.
- Use humour and emojis — be yourself
- Block time in your diary, so you embed these habits — use a habit tracker like Super Habit[2], mentioned in Chapter 3
- Split what you do and what your VA can do and delegate clear responsibility and roles
- Share articles of potential clients to your network and @mention them
- Don't get caught up in the vanity numbers of posting — 80% of the value is in direct messaging people who like and comment on your posts
- When adding a comment to someone else's post, make it memorable — you are always on show
- Look at key influencers with the same ideal client and leverage off their posts by messaging people who like and comment on their posts

The principles which apply to LinkedIn can also apply to other platforms and to email. I look to get connections on LinkedIn over to my email list as soon as possible. You can do this by giving value in a post, and they can get the rest as an opt-in on your website. LinkedIn could easily turn off the gold rush of driving organic traffic at any time, so bear this in mind.

If you are not getting responses through LinkedIn, try emails and other social channels.

We are at the cutting edge of how to maximise LinkedIn to drive more leads. Like to get more leads with LinkedIn? Email me at paul@buildlivegive.com.

---

1   http://o-dan.net/en/
2   https://www.superhabit.co/

i.iii. Book

First, I take my hat off to anyone reading this who has a book of their own. I now know how hard it is. Like many things in life, hard to do and thoroughly rewarding when done.

If you are thinking of writing a book, I can refer you to people who can help. An obvious one is Kath Walters[3], who helped me to write this book. A big thank you to Kath again. Without her guidance, this would not have been possible.

If you have a book, you can use it to build leads for your business.

Some options:

▸ Give away a free chapter in return for an email address
▸ Give away free books to open the door to clients and podcasters
▸ Give away your book at an event
▸ Give away books to joint venture partners
▸ Give away the book when speaking at an event

ii. Getting paid traffic to your business

I must declare I have a love-hate relationship with paid traffic — mainly hate. I have tried Facebook ads without success. I have not used other advertising platforms like:

▸ Instagram
▸ Google Adwords
▸ YouTube

---

3   https://kathwalters.com.au

My key learnings from my experience so far:

- ▸ Need to have a high-converting offer before you use paid traffic to boost traffic
- ▸ Get an expert to help you with the strategy
- ▸ Do some owner and/or team training to understand the basics
- ▸ You can do the implementation by yourself if you are spending less than $5,000 per month
- ▸ Use small amounts of spend to test different copy strategies
- ▸ Rotate your copy in your ad campaigns — for example, time of day
- ▸ Set up pixels on your websites for retargeting
- ▸ Use multiple social platforms — don't put all your eggs in one basket
- ▸ Facebook is a pay-to-play platform and is for B2B
- ▸ Consider desktop and mobile interfaces as clients will use a combination of both to make a decision
- ▸ Google is leveraging AI to make the platform easier to use
- ▸ Segment your audience, so you send specific messages to the right people, e.g. excluding children from targeting

I recommend using experts to avoid some of the mistakes I made with paid advertising. Book a call at www.blgmeeting.com so I can understand your objectives and direct you to the right expert.

ii.i Why is paid advertising important?

Effectively, the biggest digital platforms are Facebook, Google, YouTube and Instagram. It's all about playing where the population is. It's where people make decisions.

Personally, I haven't relied on paid advertising for leads. For most service-based businesses, it is the same. If you do the free well, it should give you the majority of your leads.

If you have a product and are more business-to-consumer (B2C), however, it could be worthwhile.

iii. Joint ventures and communities

'Free' and 'paid' traffic methods are typically where you are selling to one person. Joint ventures and communities are where you are selling to one person who can then provide leads to many.

A joint venture provides access to many ideal clients at once. Let me use the Build Live Give community as an example:

▶ Build Live Give = community of solopreneurs
▶ Expert = adds value to the members
▶ Member = has a need for the expertise

The best joint venture partnerships are based on a WIN/WIN/WIN relationship for the three parties involved.

As a community owner, one of the key benefits I bring to my members is a collection of experts they can trust. This helps me to get them a result, which I can then use to get more members.

As an expert, Meryl Johnston (mentioned in Chapter 5) provides bookkeeping services to solopreneurs using Xero accounting software. The benefit of working with Build Live Give for her is lower acquisition costs (less marketing costs to attract clients) and longer customer lifetime value (CLV), as the mentoring and support given to the members by Build Live Give provides growth in business and sustainability.

Any member can trust Bean Ninjas to do a great job and focus their time and attention on their core strengths, discussed in more detail in Chapter 9.

Joint venture partnership is about building long-term relationships. They do take time to create, and it is more of medium-term traffic and leads strategy than an immediate short-term win.

Many people give up too early on the relationship and jump from partner to partner in haste. I believe in having a few partners with deep connections.

Some of the questions to ask partners at the start of engagement include:

- ▶ What is their business win by being a partner of yours?
- ▶ What is their personal win?
- ▶ Who is their ideal client?
- ▶ What does a perfect referral look like for them?
- ▶ What does a perfect referral look like for you?
- ▶ What value can you give them first to build trust in the relationship?
- ▶ What does the commercial model look like and what is the size of the prize for them in the first 12 months?
- ▶ What routine can you put in place to get consistency in the relationship? (I prefer a regular meeting)
- ▶ What permanent fixture can you put in place into their marketing calendar, which will drive leads to your business?
- ▶ What are the terms and conditions of the partnership?
- ▶ What is the scorecard to track progress?

From experience, it is best to get a client trial as soon as possible to test the value for all three parties. I have lost significant time in the past having nice meetings which talk about the hypothetical value of the partnership without anything actually happening.

At the end of the first meeting, I ask for one of the community members to do a trial with — someone who could benefit from what I provide. Like when you are employing someone new, the interview is a nice thing to do, but a practical test is where you really get to understand if the person can deliver on what they say.

Some of my members struggle to think of how to find partners. When we spoke about your ideal client profile in Chapter 5, we spoke about who goes before you and who goes after you. This is a good place to start, to see who could be a strategic partner for you.

One of the difficulties in finding the right partner is working out if they already have a joint venture partner doing similar services to you. This information is hard to obtain, as it is normally not public. Some communities have it on their website.

We have spent significant time listing all the key communities in the world and collecting data on who their partners are. One of the benefits of our community is getting access to this information. This can save you significant time. To find out more, please go to https://buildlivegive.com/more-leads

iii.i. When should I not go into a joint venture?

When it's not a WIN/WIN/WIN. If you're just after their traffic and their clients but, you can't provide anything back in return, it won't go well. You need to ask, 'What's the win for me? But most importantly, what's the win for my partner?'

It can take a lot of time to find the right partner. One partner might end up being the right fit, but don't put all your eggs in one basket. Have options and a plan B just in case.

I had a great partner for a particular service, and it was working extremely well for all three players — well, that is what I thought. Due to a change in the partner's business model, the affiliate commission paid was not financially viable for them anymore. I had not looked at this from their perspective which, in hindsight, was a mistake on my behalf. They sent me an email saying, 'In X time period, all new referrals will not attract an affiliate commission.' This commission was coming out of their pocket, and not a margin put on to the client.

It had an impact on my financials that I didn't see coming. I also didn't have a plan B because I was too comfortable with the current arrangement.

From this experience, I learned to provide choice to members by having more than one partner for a category and also taught them to protect themselves in case something should happen.

This brings up the point of affiliate fees. An affiliate fee is when a partner gives you an amount of money for a period of time for a referral. I have a principle that the money paid to myself for referrals must come out of the partner's pocket. They are saving on the cost of acquiring a client by getting a referral from Build Live Give, so they should fund the affiliate fee. The alternative is for the client to pay a higher price — something I don't agree with. The only exception to the rule is when you white-label a service. White label is when you sell a service at the market rate, and you have someone providing the service at wholesale prices. This can work for all parties.

In the example given above, where there was no longer an affiliate fee, I would still put this partner forward as an option for the client. The end result to the client is more important in the long-term than collecting an affiliate fee. The trap some people can fall into is looking at the rate they will make on the affiliate fee and putting that before the best option for the client. This is short-sighted and not something I recommend.

I always give my members three options and let them choose what is best for them.

iii.ii. Referrals

One more traffic source which is worth mentioning, which is related to both free and joint ventures, is referrals.

There were 7,500 small businesses surveyed in North America about the single biggest way they get new clients, and 85% of them said word-of-mouth referrals. Compared to this, just 2% said radio, 1% said newspaper ads, 9% said either Google or Facebook, and 2% said through direct mail. Referrals are, by far, the number one way of driving traffic[1].

Many community members at first say: 'It's uncomfortable to ask people for referrals and I always forget to do it and I don't know when to do it'.

---

1   https://www.entrepreneur.com/article/302229

I hear you. And sometimes people give referrals to others who aren't your ideal client. If you're getting a lot of these, you haven't been specific enough on who your ideal client is so that they can refer the right people.

Have a system for asking for referrals, so it becomes simply something you do.

One of the best times to ask for a referral is when your client starts to work with you. They have gone through your sales process and know who it is best for and the result you will get them. Ask for a referral or introduction to a peer or friend.

Another time is when you do a net promoter score or feedback form, and they give you a high rating. As mentioned in the LinkedIn section, asking for recommendations is another action you can do at this time.

The most important element in getting referrals is to provide great service.

iii.iii. Are there any exceptions?

You need to have the ability to say no when it's not a good fit. Even if someone's referred to you, don't feel like you have to take them on if they're not the right client for you. Put them through your client rating mentioned in Chapter 5.

I will always look to find them someone else who can help if they are not the right fit.

ii. Converting traffic into sales

Now you've got the traffic through free and paid methods, joint ventures and referrals, it is time to convert this into sales.

As I will talk more about in Chapter 7, many solopreneurs feel uncomfortable with the word 'sales'. It can have a negative connotation.

I once heard on a podcast (I listen to so many that I can't remember the source) that 'sales' originated in Denmark and it loosely meant 'to find out where someone is at, where they wanted to go and to help them get there the best way possible'.

This is very much in line with my thoughts on sales. If you genuinely understand where the client is now and what their future desires are, and can provide them with the best option to achieve it, then you have an obligation to help them.

This reframing has helped many solopreneurs, who are givers by nature, to realise sales is simply the conversation to help achieve this end state.

You are best placed to put yourself in the shoes of your prospect and objectively assess all the options available to see which is best for them. The process of doing this should remove any ickiness when it comes to sales. Easy said than done. We will cover this in the next section.

iii. Prioritising selling

Before we cover the three habits of sales, I would like to address the elephant in the room. If you don't prioritise the time to sell, you will not have a sustainable business.

In Chapter 3, we spoke about sales being one of the Core Four activities a solopreneur must do. I mentioned that the owner of the business is best placed to sell up to $1 million in annual revenue. No matter what experience you have with sales in the past, you need to allocate time to sell. Obviously, the lack of confidence in how to sell will impact your motivation to allocate time to it.

In our group mentoring program https://buildlivegive.com/surge, we ask people to track where they spend their time each day in 30-minute blocks. As mentioned in Chapter 3, we recommend Toggl[1] to do this.

---

1   https://www.toggl.com

At the end of the week, we look at how many hours were spent on selling. Most members are shocked to realise they're spending 5-10% of their time on selling. To make matters worse, 50% of this is on sales admin — especially if they don't have a VA.

We believe that it should be closer to 25-30% of your time spent on selling and 15-20% of your time on marketing. This is excluding admin.

You need an offer that converts to have a sustainable business. The only way to know if an offer convert is to have sales conversations.

iii.i Meet Anthony

Anthony is one of our Build Live Give community members and had a stellar career at some of the biggest brand names on the planet. He left to work in consulting and recruitment, but his values didn't align with his employer's, so he started his own consulting business.

He was wearing many hats, struggling with low revenue, and just wasn't spending enough time on sales. He's great at building relationships, but the admin was tying him down. He was only spending about 10% of his time on sales.

We got him a VA to take care of some of the admin tasks that he was doing, and also to help with sales follow-up. We improved his sales scripts, so he was better at asking the right questions, and then we implemented a sales CRM system called Copper[2] to allow him to track sales.

By implementing those actions, he built up his sales muscle and ended up spending more time on sales. The more success he had through implementing these processes, the more time he wanted to spend on selling.

Now he's spending about 30% of his time on sales and, at this point, he's on track to double his revenue in 12 months.

---

2   https://www.copper.com/

iii.ii. Are there any exceptions?

If you're selling a highly automated offer, something like an online course, you're using marketing automation instead of personal selling and in this situation, you don't need to spend as much time selling.

So I have the time, how do I use it?

The importance of spending time on sales is the first part. Using your time wisely is the second phase.

Having spent 18 years working in sales at Coca-Cola and 8+ years learning from mentors and masterminds while also mentoring solopreneurs, I believe in three habits to build your capability and confidence to help prospective clients get a result.

1. Mindset
2. Skills
3. Systems

I will give you a summary of our key learnings and let you know where to find out more.

Mindset

Many solopreneurs feel uncomfortable when they think of sales. Especially if they came from a background where someone else did the selling in their previous life, and they focused on the delivery.

To the extreme, some solopreneurs avoid selling and fill their sales time with chats. They tend to talk to people they are comfortable with rather than the people who really need their help.

One of my clients, who would like to stay anonymous, was not converting conversations/chats into sales. They kept going back to the same people to have a chat, and the conversations were cordial and pleasant; however, they were not moving the needle.

When we explored it further, it became obvious there were some critical elements missing

1. There was no clear agenda

2. There was no structure to the calls

3. They were treating the call more like a coaching session and not a sales conversion

4. They spoke to the same people to avoid the issue of talking to new clients

We reframed what selling meant to them. We trained them on skills which increased their confidence. We put the systems in place to make it easy for follow-up and we put a VA in place to take care of the admin.

The biggest mind-shift change was realising; they already had all the questioning skills and abilities from their coaching experience. They had all the ingredients to be great at sales, and their self-doubt was getting in the way.

Yes, they needed to ask different questions to what they asked in a coaching call, but the basic principles were the same.

I am pleased to report they are having great success in gaining new clients. While the skills and systems were helpful, without the mindset change, it would not have happened.

Here's a list of questions I ask clients about mindset in my sales audit, which will show you how to get some help:

- ▶ What type of language do you use in sales calls? What I am looking for here is a positive language. I am trained in neuro-linguistic programming (NLP) by Smarter Selling[1] and the words you use make a significant difference to your conversations

- ▶ How do you feel when I mention the word sales? As discussed before, if you bring baggage into a sales call, it will limit the value you can give your prospective client

- ▶ What assumptions around sales can sometimes get in the way of selling? This helps uncover any further limiting beliefs

- ▶ What do clients need of you? This helps people put themselves in the shoes of the client and get out of their own head

- ▶ How good are you at listening? Give me an example. The more you can quieten the little voice of self-doubt in your head, the better you are able to listen to your prospect. If a member talks too much in a sales role play with me, it is often because they are covering up their inability to have a still mind and ask the right questions.

I am accredited by the Institute of Executive Coaching and Leadership[2] and use these skills to help you uncover the truth behind your struggles with mindset. I also have several experts I can refer you to for further development. Getting the mindset right is an essential step before moving to skills and systems. Too often, we are quick to jump to the tangible and miss the intangible.

To get specific guidance on this, please email me at paul@buildlivegive.com.

---

1   https://www.smarterselling.com.au
2   https://www.iecl.com/au

Skills

Having the right mindset is an excellent start. Now it is time to build the skills to make it easier for you.

There are two camps on skills — born or learned. I am more in favour of the latter.

When I first started to sell as a merchandiser at Coca-Cola in the early 1990s, it was 70% personality and 30% skills. The more extroverted and driven you were, typically, the better the results. I have always felt the Coca-Cola Company was at the cutting edge for sales (they used the best experts), so other companies may have relied even more on personality.

I will not bore you with the history of selling, but it's fair to say the gregarious extrovert is not always going to make the best salesperson in today's world. Personality has little to do with success. Don't get me wrong — building trust and rapport is still essential, but you don't have to be the loudest person in the room to achieve this.

The degree of knowledge and preparation a potential client has, prior to talking to you, is far greater now due to the digital age. They are better informed and the 'stretching of the truth' is no longer tolerated.

Building authentic human to human relationships is essential. As Chris Ducker[3], best selling author says: 'People buy from people.'

These are the key skills questions I ask members:

- ▶ What skills are needed to be great at sales? I have my own checklist, but I am always interested to hear what they think

- ▶ Do you qualify your prospects? I am looking for desktop research prior to the call, forms a prospect fills out prior to a call, what questions they ask and how long the call is, how they open the call and what the objective they have in the call is

---

3 https://www.chrisducker.com

- ▶ Do you have a rating system for clients? We use a points system to give a YES or NO to progress to a sales call — privileges of running your own business

- ▶ How many sales calls do you have a day, and how do you structure your time? Some people like to block time in their calendars, and others tend to be more free-flowing. The key for me is tracking the time spent. If you get the skills right, the quality will be high.

- ▶ What percentage of time do you talk in a sales call? As mentioned in the mindset above, the greater the confidence, the higher the listening. I aim for 80% listening. I keep questions to one sentence and 20-40 seconds long. I cut out all the padding and just ask the simplest of questions.

- ▶ What research do you do prior to the call? Social media and the internet are your greatest friends. I split my research into desktop research and client answers. My VAs do desktop research. If you would like an example, email me at paul@buildlivegive.com. Then we use forms to collect the information that is not public. If they aren't willing to fill in a form, they may not be serious about working together or motivated to change.

- ▶ What are the business and personal wins for a future client? At Coca-Cola, we were trained by Miller Heiman[1] in a program called The Blue Sheet. I use it every day for strategic selling (how often have you missed the life partner in a solopreneur business?). Part of the process is to uncover business and personal wins. I find personal wins are what most people miss. What will the money they make allow them to do in their personal lives? As per our mantra — build a business to fund your lifestyle and give back

- ▶ How many times to do follow up? Money is always left on the table in poor followup. Most people do one follow up; the best do 7-9. Boring messages like 'I am following up on...' is not what I am talking about here. Great quality follow-up will lift your conversion. We have some great scripts inside our Build Live Give community.

---

1   https://www.millerheimangroup.com

- What is sent after the call? Sending an email with a summary of the key points and a clear 'next steps' will increase conversions. I use templates in Copper[2] and CloudHQ for Gmail[3] which do 80% of the work for me.

- What metrics are tracked? I could write a chapter on this. Most solopreneurs are not good at tracking metrics. It is not hard to do, especially if you are using a sales CRM. If you would like to see what we track, email me at paul@buildlivegive.com.

- What is the average time it takes to make a sale? When I ask solopreneurs this question, I really get a fact-based answer. At Coca-Cola, we tracked and had KPIs to reduce the number of hours to close a sale. I don't recommend going to that extreme, but look at the total time and see how you can reduce it. Is a 12-page proposal necessary or will one page do? We use Better Proposals[4], and it gives you analytics on how long a future client spends in a proposal. How short the time is may shock you!

- What do you do for existing clients? Up to now, we have focused on new clients to double revenue. But if you have existing clients, there are offers you can provide them to increase revenue. How to work out the offers and who to target is called account management. With all clients I have worked with, this is a hidden treasure chest. You already have good trust and a track record of delivering. Using some of the skills and tools that I learned at Coca-Cola will bring great results for your clients and more revenue for you.

- How do you set pricing? We covered this in Chapter 6. If you missed it, I recommend going back and reading it.

- What is the mix of one-off and recurring revenue? Many members work on an hour or project rate and miss the benefits of recurring. Clients like recurring because it gives them certainty for forecasting costs and it gives you the consistency of revenue.

---

2   http://www.prosperworks.com/?utm_source=R-ScaleMyEmpire
3   https://www.cloudhq.net/g_suite
4   https://betterproposals.io/partners#_r_paul11

Systems

We have now covered mindset and skills, which are the building blocks of successful sales. Too often, I see people start with systems and miss the fundamentals. Getting the order right is very important.

You may be clamping up around now and want to flick past this section to the next chapter. I get it. Systems can come with trepidation. I encourage you to resist the urge and read this section. It is not at all techie.

The great news — what I will recommend here is all about the ease of use. Think about how we use apps on our phone — sales systems are no different.

When I worked at Coca-Cola, we had over 152 different sales CRMs across the globe. The user experience was average, and the time and cost to make modifications and customisations were painful. Companies like Coca-Cola saw their sales systems as a clear point of difference to smaller competitors. This is less of a case due to the rise of software as a service (SAAS).

I still have many friends in corporate who are envious of the tools available to solopreneurs. The speed, user experience and cost are definitely advantageous to smaller and nimble businesses.

Scott from Scale My Empire[1], mentioned in Chapter 5, advises our community members on what sales and operations systems are best. Scott started with solopreneurs, and he is a world expert. He tests them all and really knows his stuff. For what I don't know about systems, we have Scott as a backup.

---

1   http://scalemyempire.com/

What do I mean by sales systems?

When I talk about systems, I will focus on sales CRMs. Back in Chapter 3, I mentioned the difference between marketing CRM and sales CRM. Before I go into some tips on picking the right sales CRM for your business, I will call out the elephant in the room. This has to do with using Google Sheets or Excel spreadsheets as your sales CRM.

Many solopreneurs believe a spreadsheet is a good option until they grow their revenue. I hear them, but I don't agree. There are some great free sales CRM like HubSpot[2], which runs rings around using a sheet. There is a limited downside, other than the initial migration of data, to using a great free tool like this. If the migration is going to be a challenge, then I recommend running the two and only adding the new clients and information in the sales CRM. This is easier than you think.

For the paid versions with more features, the monthly investment is typically USD$49-79 per month. The opportunity cost of missing one sale because of poor follow-up will always outweigh the cost.

Excel was never intended to be a sales CRM, and it should not be used this way. I have not had a solopreneur go back to Excel once they see the power of a sales CRM.

Okay, I will get off my soapbox and share our learnings on how to pick the right sales CRM:

▶ The type of sales — this sounds obvious, however high volume outbound leads are different from nurturing existing clients.

---

2   https://www.hubspot.com/

▶ What email provider — most people are on Gmail, and there are sales CRMs better integrated with Gmail. The same is true for Outlook. You want to be able to scrape your data from your emails directly into your sales CRM

▶ Customer lifetime value (CLV) — the larger the value, the more budget for a sales CRM

▶ What peers use — having the same sales CRM as fellow community members will help with shared learnings

▶ Feature set — this can open a can of worms as it can be very confusing to compare feature sets. There are some sites which help like GetApp[1] and G2 Crowd[2]. I recommend emailing me to help you sort through this maze paul@buildlivegive.com

▶ Mobile app — the quality of the mobile app and how full-featured it is compared to the desktop version

▶ Reporting — what is standard and what it allows you to integrate with

▶ Workflow automation — does it have the ability to reduce time with integrations?

▶ Native integrations — I know this is getting a little technical, so I'll give you a simple example. Copper Sales CRM[3] has native integration with Mailchimp[4] and Xero[5]. This means you can see the information and push information from Copper to Xero, saving you time.

1   https://www.getapp.com
2   https://www.g2.com/
3   http://www.prosperworks.com/?utm_source=R-ScaleMyEmpire
4   https://mailchimp.com/
5   https://www.xero.com

Summary

In this chapter, we've learned three important ways of driving traffic:

1. Free

2. Paid

3. Joint venture

We also spoke about referrals.

We then talked about how you convert that traffic to happy clients through:

1. Mindset

2. Skills

3. Systems

The key actions under marketing are:

Free

▶ Decide what podcasts to go on and whether to use valet service or not

▶ Investigate setting up your own podcast

▶ Get on LinkedIn and take actions on profile, posting, relationships, sales navigator and killer tips

▶ Decide if you will write a book, and if you already have one, see how you can promote it more. It is not a launch; it is an asset to leverage

Paid

▶ Seek help from an expert

▶ Use multi-platform methods to drive traffic

▶ Take actions based on the tips given

Joint venture

- ▶ Be patient
- ▶ Realise that less is more
- ▶ Do due diligence and look for WIN/WIN
- ▶ Have regular routines
- ▶ Get a trial happening ASAP
- ▶ Have a plan B

Referrals

- ▶ Put a system in place

The key actions under sales are:

Mindset

- ▶ Reframe what sales mean
- ▶ Prioritise time
- ▶ Assess your abilities against the questions and seek help

Skills

- ▶ Know that sales skills can be taught
- ▶ Assess your abilities against the questions and seek help

Systems

- ▶ Stop using sheets and start to use a sales CRM
- ▶ Get help in picking the right one for you
- ▶ Know that you don't need to migrate all data. You can run parallel systems and put only the new information into your sales CRM

The reason this chapter is one of the two longest (the other being Chapter 3, on personal effectiveness) is a testament to the importance of attracting leads and converting them in a solopreneurs business.

You don't have to do this all by yourself, as we have several experts who you can trust to deliver you results.

Avoiding improving your ability to market and sell is harming you and your business. Once you learn and gain confidence in this area, you can transfer this into any business you run.

Chapter 8

Rapid Growth Driver 5 — High-Performing Teams

Introduction

This chapter is about building a high-performing team to help give exceptional results for clients while helping you to maintain your lifestyle.

Implementing the four rapid growth drivers mentioned in the previous chapters will get you results — more clients and more work. Building a high-performing team helps you to avoid burnout and to let people down.

Many solopreneurs get uneasy when I mention the word team. You may have left your previous role because you didn't want to manage a large team of people. I totally understand. I have led teams of up to 150 people and know what challenges come with it.

Our version of a team is different from the traditional model. The traditional model is people working in the same office location and the majority working full-time.

We have a different view, made up of three areas:

1. Direct remote team — full-time people working for you, e.g. Virtual Assistants
2. Freelancers — part-time people working for you, e.g. podcast editors
3. Experts — specialists on an as needs basis, e.g. web developers and bookkeepers

They are all part of a team of people helping you achieve amazing results, regardless of where they work or how they are paid.

But remote in location doesn't mean your leadership style is remote.

All of my experience from working at the Coca-Cola Company — 126 years old and over 800,000 employees globally — and my knowledge of working with solopreneurs over the last seven years have been combined to provide a pathway for you to build a remote team that will help you handle the increased workload coming down the line.

Our world is going digital, but humans still like to work with humans. Potential and current clients want to talk to the owner of the business. As the business scales, the demands stretch a solopreneur too thin. A team releases this pressure. As mentioned in Chapter 6 on non-negotiables, you need to set your lifestyle first and then build a business which supports it.

Many solopreneurs leave a job because they work too many hours, don't see their family and don't have the lifestyle they wanted. This may resonate with you. A team helps avoid falling into the same trap. As stated on several occasions in this book, I recommend starting with a VA as your first hire.

Why have a high performing team?

Let me give you an example. We talked about Scott from Scale My Empire in Chapter 5. Scott was a solo consultant, helping people sort out their tech. A very smart guy. Customers loved him, but he ran out of time to implement and ended up working way too many hours. He was working from home; however, he was not spending time with his young family.

His first hire was a VA to remove the admin tasks from his plate and do sales follow-up. Then we hired project managers to do the implementation. This allowed Scott to focus on what he was best at — strategy.

We did a strengths assessment using Gallup's CliftonStrengths 34[1] and the areas he was not strong at or didn't have the skills for, we brought in experts. This included a:

▶ Marketing consultant
▶ LinkedIn expert
▶ Web developer

---

1   https://www.gallup.de/182696/clifton-strengthsfinder.aspx

- ▸ Content writer
- ▸ Graphic designer
- ▸ Bookkeeper
- ▸ Accountant

Scott's business grew, and the hours he worked declined.

We worked with Scott to tailor his leadership style to leverage this remote team.

The key elements were:

- ▸ Culture and engagement
- ▸ Team development
- ▸ Team systems
- ▸ Project Management
- ▸ Automation

We will cover each in more detail now.

i. Culture and engagement

Large companies attract job seekers based on brand, remuneration, career progression and training. Solopreneurs, as a general rule, find it hard to complete on these. What solopreneurs can bring to the table is an attractive culture.

i.i. What key elements make a great culture?

The first is around your story. Why are you doing what you are doing? What is your purpose? What's the vision for your business? What are the values and behaviours and are they aligned to the job seekers?

There are also symbols that define a culture. One example, from my old corporate days, were carpark spots marked 'Reserved for MD'. Another is senior leaders flying first class when the team fly economy.

Solopreneurs tend to be more inclusive and less status-driven.

i.ii. Meet Nick

Nick is one of our members who are in a very competitive space — through Oakvale Homes & Development[1] he does house remodelling in the United States of America.

There's a skill shortage over there and, he wanted to get the best-skilled people. What he did was articulate his culture, which the whole company lived by. This allowed him to attract better quality people. Some of his competitors hadn't defined their culture and how it benefits job seekers. Nick was able to attract and recruit the best people because of his well-defined culture and his ability to live it.

i.iii. How do I build the right culture?

There are eight areas of what makes a great culture.

1. Our guiding principles
2. Stories
3. Values
4. Behaviours
5. Symbols
6. Team
7. Routines & Rituals
8. Leaders

To help illustrate this, I will use Build Live Give as an example.

---

1   https://www.oakvalehome.com/

Our guiding principles

- ▶ Be honest about today and have a clear vision for the future
- ▶ Community members are at the centre of all that we do — we shine through their success
- ▶ Don't accept the status quo, make recommendations and challenge what we do
- ▶ 10% of time learning — be the world's best at a skill you love doing which benefits our clients
- ▶ Do it once and create repeating tasks
- ▶ World-class SOPs
- ▶ Flat open structure
- ▶ Deliver on commitments, and if you can't, please explain why ahead of time

Stories

- ▶ My journey of leaving corporate to manage my health and spend time with family — personal life comes first; business life comes second
- ▶ Success stories of members travelling the world whilst working

Values

- ▶ High performance
- ▶ Integrity
- ▶ Exceptional communication

Behaviours

- ▶ Proactive
- ▶ Attentive to detail
- ▶ Curious

Symbols

- ▶ We give to charity
- ▶ Open door (metaphorically speaking)
- ▶ No rank debriefs

Team

- ▸ Based all over the world
- ▸ All work from home
- ▸ Every team member has a personal development plan

Routines & Rituals

- ▸ Weekly huddle chaired by different team member each month
- ▸ We talk about personal wins every week in the huddle
- ▸ Work in progress meetings each week
- ▸ Team social catchup every month
- ▸ Performance reviews every trimester
- ▸ Every Friday there is a message from Paul to the team
- ▸ Random acts of kindness and rewarding the team

Leaders

- ▸ Treat the team like you would like to be treated yourself
- ▸ Stretch the team to achieve more than they believe is possible in themselves
- ▸ Play by the same rules as everyone else
- ▸ Deliver on your commitments
- ▸ Back the team when you need to

i.iv. What barriers might I come up against when building a team culture?

A solopreneur's strength is the ability to be nimble and act in the moment. This can sometimes cause a focus on the short-term over the long-term. It is easy to defer the development of conversations based on the immediacy of the day. Excuses like 'culture are for large companies and not for small companies like ours' can inhibit one's ability to attract and retain great people.

Clients can also challenge you to take shortcuts and go against your agreed culture. The pressure to have revenue can be challenging.

Stay true to the culture you've created. This is something only a true leader can do.

i.v. How to engage people?

As stated in Forbes[1], 'Employee engagement is the emotional commitment the employee has to the organization and its goals.'

Engagement is about how much someone enjoys working for a business and if they would refer someone else to work there. The team should be excited, enthusiastic and working productively in business, possibly going the extra mile when they can.

Team members not engaged tend to do the bare minimum. It is easy to see it in a small team, but when they are remote, it can be camouflaged.

One way to measure engagement is to use engagement tools like 6Q[2] and Peakon[3]. They provide monthly analytics on the team's engagement. There are typically 12 questions to fill out each month. There are a great dashboard and the chance for team members to leave qualitative comments.

Let me give an example of how we used it with our team of 30 people in the Philippines. We thought our team was going really well and, from the outside, everything looked great. We were based in Australia and visited every quarter.

Having done employment opinion scores at Coca-Cola every two years, I wanted something more immediate. We implemented the Peakon tool monthly.

---

1   https://www.forbes.com/sites/kevinkruse/2012/06/22/employee-engagement-what-and-why/#640f57a47f37
2   https://www.6q.io/
3   https://peakon.com/

When we got the results back, to say we got a big shock was an understatement. We had a manager whose management style created a toxic environment for the team. They upward-managed well, and my team in the Philippines culturally didn't want to say anything. Eventually, we would have picked up on the low engagement, but Peakon brought to notice of it forward.

We investigated further and found out the situation was untenable. We needed to make a hard call, and it was time for the team lead to go.

I find these tools especially important if you are leading a remote workforce with different cultural norms. I am not a supporter of tracking remote workers through time or screen-tracking software. I ask myself the simple question: 'Would I want to work that way? Would that bring the best out of me?' If the answer is 'no', then why should it be fair for anyone else in the team?

If you're using a really short-term freelancer, then these tools are probably overkill. If it is a longer-term expert or contractor, I highly recommend it.

Some other options to consider:

- ▶ Culture Amp[4]
- ▶ 15Five[5]
- ▶ Officevibe[6]
- ▶ TINYpulse Engage[7]

I am happy to help you set this up. Email me at paul@buildlivegive.com

Before you send out the questionnaire, it is best to give the right context for it:

- ▶ Make it very clear that the survey is anonymous and you have no way of finding out individual results

---

4   https://www.cultureamp.com/
5   https://www.15five.com/
6   https://www.officevibe.com/
7   https://www.tinypulse.com/engage

- Let them know what you are going to do with the results and how you plan to implement the findings
- Tell them how the survey will directly benefit them
- Stress why their honesty is so important
- Plan the debriefing sessions
- Inform them how long it will take and the frequency of future questionnaires

Once the results come back, work directly with the team to summarise the key learnings. I then recommend asking the team to come up with solutions to improve the areas which need the most work. Depending on the size of the team, an independent facilitator running a session can work well as well. I have done this for many of my clients.

The role of the leader is to resource the plan then and have it on the top of their agenda.

Having absorbed myself in Filipino culture over the past seven years, I know they tend to avoid confrontation. It is rare for an employee to tell their leader exactly what they think, as they don't want to offend them.

If your team is too small to benefit from these platforms, you can still benefit from engagement surveys. Starting with a free service like Typeform[1] or Google Form[2] and using the questions can be a good place to start. The key is to make sure it is anonymous, which is harder with these options than the paid platforms.

ii. Team development

Having a great team can have a massively positive impact on your business and your personal life. Building capability is a two-way street. When I completed my coaching accreditation at the Institute of Executive

1   https://www.typeform.com

2   https://www.google.com.au/forms/about

Coaching and Leadership (IECL)[3], I learnt about above and below the line, which I briefly touched on in Chapter 4.

Above the line is what you can do to develop a team member and below the line is what they can do. At Coca-Cola, there was a healthy debate on where the line was drawn. Some believed development was more the responsibility of the individual, while others felt it was the responsibility of management. Personally, I saw merit in both approaches.

I was very lucky to have some amazing development at Coca-Cola. In addition, I did my own development. Like a seesaw, it should find a natural balance. At Build Live Give we like to have both. Our behaviours of proactive and curiosity, as mentioned before, support this.

I have found great people like to be developed — stretched beyond their current capability. If not, they get bored, lose engagement and, in the worst-case scenario, stay and underperform. As a solopreneur, the team can become like family, and it can be hard to let people go. By developing people, this reduces the chance of this.

At Coca-Cola, we had individual development plans (IDPs). After a performance review, a key strength was identified and focused on.

For example, it might be communication as a skill or competency. A plan on how to further develop this skill was agreed with yourself and your leader. This was called strength-based development. There were many occasions where leaders looked at an area where someone was not strong and looked to develop this. As a general rule, this seemed to be less successful.

ii.i. A real-life example

I will give you an example. I had a team member who was incredibly strategic and creative. On the flip side, their planning and organisation skills let them down. Previous leaders had invested enormous energy and dollars in trying to develop their planning and organisational skills. I felt like this was like trying to put a square peg in a round hole.

3   https://www.iecl.com

I asked them to do some personality profiling. The tool we used was the Herrmann Brain Dominance Indicator https://www.herrmann.com.au/the-hbdi. It showed their natural preference was significantly weighted to strategy and that when under pressure, they avoided planning and organising. As a certified HBDI trainer, you are taught the opposite quadrants typically oppose. This could not be truer for this person.

I worked with them to leverage their strengths, and their engagement and output afterwards were extraordinary.

On the planning and organisation front, I got my executive assistant to cover this for them. A WIN/WIN/WIN.

ii.ii. How do you bring it to life?

Once the skill or competency is decided, set aside 30 minutes per month, one-on-one, to talk about the progress made.

The team member leads the conversation and takes responsibility for their own development. The leader's role is to hold them accountable and provide resources — usually time and money. The day-to-day work conversations should be left at the door. It's purely about their development. It's like planting an orange tree. It takes about seven years to mature. The investment put in today will give rewards down the track.

At Coca-Cola, we used the 70/20/10 rule as a guide for development plans:

- ▶ 70% on-job training
- ▶ 20% internal resources
- ▶ 10% external

Let me talk you through an example. Names have been changed in this section.

Betty is one of our team members and very good at attention to detail. This includes writing standard operating procedures (SOPs). There were other people in the team responsible for this ,but their attention to detail was not a strength.

I saw it as a lost opportunity. So I moved some social media tasks (which she didn't love anyway) off her and allocated her the responsibility of SOPs across the team. The 70/20/10 looked like this:

- ▶ 70% on-job — review all SOPs and improve them.
- ▶ 20% internal — she gave the SOP to a colleague to implement and all the gaps discovered were closed. She also spent time learning other roles to refine the SOPs, which reduced the risk of knowledge sitting with only one team member.
- ▶ 10% external — she did an external course with Scott from Scale My Empire and Ari Meisel's team from Less Doing[1]. Both are global experts on SOPs for solopreneurs.

We reviewed her monthly progress in the one on one meeting. The quality of the SOPs improved significantly, and Betty gained great confidence and enjoyment.

ii.iii. This sounds too easy?

This all sounds great in theory. However, having done this for 26+ years now, I know how hard it is.

There's always burning client issues or revenue chasing to be done, or something that will get in the road. That's what happened in corporate, and it's even more challenging as a solopreneur. There tend to be fewer cheques and balances unless you have a great mentor or coach. If people are the most important part of a business, then it has to be a must-do task.

There's a great book called The Balanced Scorecard by Robert S. Kaplan and David P. Norton[2]. It talks about getting the four areas right:

---

1   https://lessdoing.com
2   https://www.balancedscorecard.org/BSC-Basics/About-the-Balanced-Scorecard

- ▸ Financial
- ▸ Customer
- ▸ People
- ▸ internal processes

These are critical to making your business a success. Too often, we focus on lag measures of finance and forget to focus on the lead measures of people.

iii. Team systems

The word 'systems' and solopreneurs can be like oil and water. I know, for me, when I left corporate, I wanted to be free. Anything that looked like systems or structures, I avoided like the plague. Did this cost me growth? For sure. Would I do it differently? You bet.

What I will take you through here are the minimum systems you need to run your business from anywhere. As we covered in personal systems in Chapter 3, systems these days are much easier than ever before.

Most of the systems used by solopreneurs are the same for the team. How do we know this? We have spent the last eight years working with hundreds of solopreneurs to test and measure. All of the learnings are from practical experience.

Solopreneurs can run a $10,000 a month business which is predominantly dependent on them from their home with few systems.

To double revenue to $20,000+, it is nearly impossible not to have the right people and the right systems. If achieved, the cash taken out of the business is increased because of the higher labour component needed. Let me explain.

In most service-based businesses, labour is the largest expense. This is definitely the case for solopreneurs. I often hear solopreneurs miss 'the money [they] make' as they probably don't account for their cost of providing the service. At Coca-Cola, you had to know your numbers. I was involved in acquiring billion-dollar businesses that all came down to the numbers. If this is not a strength for you, I am happy to help. Simply email me at paul@ buildlivegive.com.

Now I will give some examples of what numbers you should track in your business, directly to do with your largest cost — people.

I like to set a target for direct staff costs to be at maximum, 18% of revenue. What does this mean? For example, if the monthly cost of the direct team is $6,000 and the monthly revenue is $33,000 — then $33,000 divided by $6,000 = 18%. The lower the percentage, the better.

A way of reducing this percentage is by getting direct staff to do more in less time. If what they are doing are the right activities, the revenue will go up. One thing to watch here is when the ratio is coming down because the solopreneur is doing too much work and not paying themselves. I track this in the solopreneurs drawings to revenue ratio.

Many solopreneurs don't pay themselves for the work they do — they don't value their own time. There is an opportunity cost of time, and it needs to be factored in. The way it is calculated is revenue divided by drawings, as shown in the direct staff example above. I like to target 24%. You add the most value and carry the most risk; therefore you should be rewarded accordingly.

The other labour component is the use of experts, which we discussed in Chapter 3. I like this to be 12% of revenue.

So the moral of the story is: the better the system, the greater the effectiveness of the team and the higher the cash coming from the business.

The other factor is the ability to work from anywhere. The fewer systems used, the fewer freedom. As mentioned in Chapter 1, I was able to work from the hospital during my dialysis and transplant because of my systems. Fortunately for you, work from anywhere should be more glamorous and involve fun things like travel.

So this covers why let's now cover how.

The four elements for building team systems are:

▸ Platforms

▸ Standard Operating Procedures

▸ Project Management

▸ Automation

iii.i. Platforms

In Chapter 3, we covered the key platforms we recommend you use as a solopreneur. I recommend reading this again if you skipped it previously. I will not go over them again, however, I will mention some tips to make it work best for you and the team.

▸ Platforms work best when everyone is on the same page — for example, I have at least ten ways I can be contacted by my team, but I nominated Voxer[1] as the only way to message me for immediate response. This is not easy to do, but it is hugely beneficial for all when it is clear and specific. Not draining your brain by worrying if something is being missed helps your effectiveness

▸ What about people not in your company? Now, this can be a little tricky as experts may have different preferred platforms to yours. I like them to use ours, and in many cases, they are one and the same, so this is OK. Where different, I either ask for ours to be used or get my team to update ours using the inputs for theirs. Give and take and pragmatic decision-making helps sort this through

▸ One key user for each platform — I nominate one key user who's role is to own the platform and train the team to get the consistency of performance. Left to the group, it will be inconsistent and create inefficiencies

▸ Hire in help — for our core platforms; we hire experts to fast-track our learnings. Get them to do an audit first. At worst, this can be

---

1   https://www.voxer.com/

implemented by your team. If they are very good, then hire them to implement

▶ Join user groups — there are several platform user groups where questions can be asked and answered. It's a great way to add value and, in some cases, could be a lead channel as well.

▶ Plan B — have a system backup in case something should happen to the platform. Also, have a plan B for the key user in case they leave the business.

▶ Usage reports — track usage reports to see who needs help in training or adoption of the platform.

If you would like to find out more email me at paul@buildlivegive.com.

iii.ii. Standard operating procedures (SOPs)

As soon as I mention these words, most solopreneurs head for the hills — me too! You can probably feel the tension as you're reading this right now. The word SOP can irk people, especially right-brained solopreneurs, with lots of creative ideas.

But I'm here to say, after many years of running my own businesses and advising hundreds of other solopreneurs, that SOPs work. There's a reason why large businesses have them.

There are ways to remove the boredom and pain of creating and implementing SOPs so that they become value-adding.

SOPs work because they give clarity on what to do. I know that sounds obvious, but so often, in a small team, there's high risk because the SOP sits in someone's head and if they were to leave then all hell would break loose.

It's important to get SOPs right so that clients get a wonderful and consistent experience. Extending client lifetime value (CLV) is a great way of making more cash to fund your lifestyle. The greater the client churn, the greater the need for client acquisition, which drains cash. Down the track, options of licensing, franchising or even selling the business are easier if SOPs are in place.

But the core reason is business continuity. In corporate, business continuity plans are standard practice, typically learned from past poor experiences. The test is this: if you took four weeks out of your business or one of the key staff left, would the business run successfully? If the answer is no, SOPs can help.

I can already hear you saying, 'If I start implementing SOPs, I'm missing out on selling time.' I get it. There will be an investment in time to get the ideas out of the solopreneur's head, which will impact sales time. In saying that, I am sure there are other activities which could be stopped to focus on sales.

It's hard NOT to take the short-term option. But really, what you're doing here is building a business and not a job. If solopreneurs want a job, then don't have SOPs. If they want to build a business, then SOPs help facilitates this.

Treating everyone like a robot by implementing SOPs so structured that people get bored and disengaged is taking it too far. Have enough structure that they're clear on what they do, but not to the 'nth' degree where they get bored by it.

Macquarie Bank's[1] tagline used to be 'Freedom Within a Framework', and I think that's such a great way of putting it. You need a clear framework, but you've got a bit of freedom around that.

Here are some tips when creating SOPs:

▸ Have a team member responsible for SOPs — if you are just starting out, a VA can play this role

▸ The person doing the process should be the person to create the first draft of the SOP. If it is the solopreneur, they can do the task and record it on their screen with tools like Dubb[2]. Some solopreneurs in our community have recorded audio and got it transcribed with a service like Rev[3] and Otter[4]

1   https://www.macquarie.com
2   https://dubb.com/?refer_code=orSGEv
3   https://www.rev.com
4   https://otter.ai/

▸ Have a standard template for SOPs — if you would like to see ours, go to https://buildlivegive.com/book-resources

▸ Get a third party who has no prior knowledge of the process to implement the SOP — many of our members use family for this.

▸ After this, the key user fixes the non-technical components and works with the person doing the process for the technical fixes

▸ Store all the SOP in one place — I recommend this to be electronic. We use Asana and have the SOP document link in there for ease of reference

▸ Create checklists for implementing the SOP — again; we have this in Asana, so the SOP is part of every working day

▸ Hire a third party who specializes in setting up SOPs if there is slow or no progress. Email me at paul@buildlivegive.com for a list of recommendations.

▸ Have a priority list of SOPs to work on. Not all processes are made equal. Typically this is related to revenue generation or client satisfaction

▸ Make it a non-negotiable as a leader. You need to practise what you preach.

▸ Accept they will not be perfect the first time. They are a continual work in progress.

iv. Project management

Project management is a term most past employees are familiar with. The definition in Wikipedia is:

'Project management is the practice of initiating, planning, executing, controlling, and closing the work of a team to achieve specific goals and meet specific success criteria at the specified time.'

For many solopreneurs, it less painful than SOPs but not by much. It sits in the same family and is not a strength.

In the definition of a team, mentioned previously, most solopreneurs will have a combination of direct employees working remotely, experts and specialist freelancers. Keeping up with all the moving parts can be complex to manage.

Labour is your largest cost for most service-based businesses, as mentioned above. This could be as high as 50% of revenue. How well people work together will have a significant impact on profit and cashflow.

iv.i. Let me show you an example

When we launched our Build Live Give membership in November 2017, we had a project manager, our VAs, an agency with their team and a web developer all working on it simultaneously. They were all remote. All in all, we had about twelve people, including myself. Within a month, we took something from scratch to a full-blown membership launch.

We appointed one person as a project manager, and then we implemented Asana[1] to manage the project. We could see the action in real-time and combined this with a weekly work-in-progress (WIP) meeting. The meetings were to remove any of the roadblocks that came up when tasks were behind schedule. Within Asana, the project updates and resource allocation was handled. It also tracked progress to milestones and held people accountable.

We delivered a successful project. Without the project manager and the platform, we would not have achieved this result.

However, if you're just going to do something one-off and you'll never do it again, project management is overkill.

Here are some tips to help implement project management:
- ▸ Have a clear project scope at the start — if the objectives are not crystal clear at the beginning, and have buy-ins, the chances of

success are low. This needs to be done by the solopreneur and cannot be delegated to someone else. It needs to align to the overall plan for the business

▶ Part of this scope is the budget — it is hard to calculate the budget

▶ The project scope needs to be over-communicated, once is not enough

▶ Have a project kick-off meeting and ask each member to summarise their personality profile, learning styles, and how they like to work. Resources can be found in Chapter 4 on VA onboarding

▶ The people 'doing' should not be the project manager. In the Build Live Give membership launch example, we used a project manager (one of my team members) to oversee the project. They had a clear brief and mandate and had time to do it. Combining the 'doing' and project management, in my experience, doesn't work.

▶ Have one platform that everyone agrees to use. This sounds easier than in practice. If there are multiple platforms, have a VA pull all the info into one. I am happy to help work through this. Send me an email at paul@buildlivegive.com.

▶ Have clear escalation rules when the project is off-track. In theory, the escalation should go to the weekly WIP meeting. In reality, this is not the case. There need to be official and unofficial rules for escalation. Listing typical scenarios of what might go wrong in advance, and how to overcome them, makes for smoother sailing

▶ Have a plan B — the assumption that everything will go to plan is more likely incorrect than correct. So what happens? What are the contingencies, and when should they be initiated?

▶ No rank debrief — in Chapter 8, we spoke about the importance of this. At the conclusion of the project, take the learnings and apply to upcoming projects.

v. Automation

When I worked at Coca-Cola, we were always looking for ways to automate people-based activities and improve efficiency, while also giving more time for people to focus on what they do best.

Coca-Cola didn't always get this right. When it became purely about cost, it often backfired. It was hard to measure the full impact of cutting costs.

Where it did work well was by using robots in production and warehousing — automating the delivery scheduling, automating financial reporting, etc.

The same principles used by a USD $146 billion company can apply to your business. As mentioned in Chapter 3, solopreneurs have unlimited access to technology to automate parts of the business.

v.i. Relatable example

Many solopreneurs are time-poor and also need to dedicate more time to sales. A typical tension and one outlined frequently throughout this book.

So, how do you find the time? One way is to reduce the time it takes to book appointments. By using a scheduling tool like Book Like a Boss[1] it can automate the process and save you, your VA and your client time. This time can be better utilised on higher valued tasks.

v.ii Integrations

I like to challenge my team to add up the hours it takes them to do a core task in the business and see how they can halve it using automation. The automation can be within the platform, or it can be by using a third party

---

1   https://partners.booklikeaboss.com/709.html

connecting software like Zapier[2] and Integromat[3] and have two different platforms sharing data.

The opportunities are endless. The key reason why we do this, other than increased cash flow, is hiring. The greatest risk for any solopreneur is making the right hire. I can't tell you how many bad hires I have made over the years — within both corporate and my own businesses.

Humans are humans, and when life throws a curveball, people handle it differently. Hiring and retaining great people is really hard. One way to reduce the risk of a bad hire is to do less hiring.

By automating, the people hours to deliver should go down. As revenue increases, the same number of people can do more. It is natural to look to hire first — I get it. I recommend to automating first, to see if you really need more people.

So here are some tips on automating:

▶ Target the processes which are essential to your business and have a large labour component, e.g. client on-boarding. A marketing automation software like Active Campaign[4] can automate the email sequences to reduce the need for labour

▶ Look at your core platforms first — for us; it is Copper[5] for sales CRM and Asana[6] for project management. What can happen natively (built into the platform, e.g. Asana repeating tasks) and what can happen through a third-party tool like Integromat?

▶ Get an expert to fast-track your learning for automations. Unless there is internal capability, it's best to buy it in

▶ Appoint a key user in the team. Their responsibility is to build the SOPs and guidelines for the business and to train the team

2   https://zapier.com
3   https://www.integromat.com/en
4   https://www.activecampaign.com
5   http://www.prosperworks.com/?utm_source=R-ScaleMyEmpire
6   http://www.asana.com

- ▸ Allocate time each week in everyone's diaries to focus on automation. This is ongoing and best to be embedded in the culture of the business
- ▸ Have repeatable tasks to check the automations as they can break, and the alerts from the integration company are not always accurate.

Summary

Through this chapter, we've learned that developing high performing teams need work and structure. We've also talked about the five key elements to implement to improve the performance of a team.

- ▸ Culture and engagement
- ▸ Team development
- ▸ Team systems
- ▸ Project Management
- ▸ Automation

Culture and engagement — elements to implement:

- ▸ Our guiding principles
- ▸ Stories
- ▸ Values
- ▸ Behaviours
- ▸ Symbols
- ▸ Team
- ▸ Routines & Rituals
- ▸ Leaders

Engagement

- ▸ Implement engagement scores and tools
- ▸ Tell the team the why

Team Development
- Above and below the line
- IDPs
- Strengths
- Monthly meetings
- 70/20/10

Team systems
- If you double your business, you will need systems
- Know your numbers
- Use systems to reduce people costs

Platforms
- Nominate the key user
- Get help with an audit and implementation plan
- Set up SOPs

Project Management
- Pick a platform
- Have a dedicated PM
- Follow the tips

Automation
- Start with the right end in mind
- Automate to reduce labour as a percentage of revenue
- Reduce the risk of hiring
- Key user and make it a routine
- Get some help

The time put in at the outset to build your high-performing team will be paid back to you in spades. Don't wait too long. If you want a job, I recommend you work for someone else — be it a contractor or full-time.

If you want to build a sustainable business which can fund your lifestyle, without working ridiculous hours, build a team.

In the next chapter, we'll go through some real-life examples of how we've implemented these Five Rapid Growth Drivers to help solopreneurs to build, live, and give.

Chapter 9

Case studies

Meryl from Bean Ninjas

My entrepreneurial story

I am an accountant by background and training. Back in 2010, I was living in Melbourne and working in a big accounting firm, BDO. Then I moved to Queensland for lifestyle reasons. I worked at a couple of different places, including Queensland Airports which owns and operates various airports and air division companies. I soon fell back into a pattern of working late nights and weekends as an employee at a big company. I'd just received a promotion, which was exciting, but it was also even more work. And I thought, 'What am I doing? I've moved to Queensland for the lifestyle, and I'm repeating the same patterns.'

And it was then that I left that role. I had nothing to go to. I travelled overseas for a couple of months. I started a consulting business, but that didn't align with my values.

And that was what inspired me to start Bean Ninjas, which is a bookkeeping company that serves entrepreneurs and solopreneurs who are changing how we live in the world.

The Build Live Give Moment

I knew it was absolutely the right business for me, but I quickly ran into challenges, which is when I joined the Build Live Give community. I bought out my former business partner and focused on creating systems and improving the profitability of different customers. I had hard decisions to make around different team members — some restructures there. Being part of the Build Live Give community and talking these issues through was really helpful.

In the latter part of 2017, I was working on a deal for investment in the business. I spoke one-on-one with Paul, which was really helpful in understanding the risks and aspects I needed to consider when bringing an investor in (especially having recently been through an experience with buying out a previous business partner).

Because I already had a relationship with Paul, I knew his background — some coaches haven't actually done 'it': They haven't had a senior role in a global business and then left to build their own business. That is important to me in any kind of coaching environment that the coach has a track record. I was also connected with some of the people in the group, like Scott and Anton, so I knew that I would benefit out of it. We had our initial calls, and I liked the frameworks Paul talked about. They aligned with what I was trying to do with my business — create processes to create freedom around my lifestyle as well as running a successful business.

Build

Rapid Growth Driver 1 — Personal Effectiveness

I have done a lot of work on effectiveness. Recently on a group call, I mentioned I had a lot on. Paul asked, 'Well, what could you cut out?' It was a simple question, but I went about cutting everything out of my calendar for three weeks, which meant I could focus on some massive projects in the business and get them done in a short amount of time. It also made me question whether those things could be cut permanently. That's a good approach to effectiveness; rather than trying to do things faster, can I cut some tasks entirely?

Rapid Growth Driver 2 — Ideal Client

Defining my ideal client made a huge difference to my business. When we first started Bean Ninjas, we tried to serve everyone. So we had tradesmen, signwriters, digital agencies, eCommerce, restaurants. It was very difficult to serve those clients because they all require different bookkeeping add-ons. And bookkeeping processes are different for different industries. It was difficult to clarify our marketing messaging because they had different paying ports too.

About halfway through 2016, a year into the business, we looked at our most profitable customers by industry, who we liked working with and who valued what we were offering. We identified that businesses that were running online were the ideal clients for us. Since then, we've been focusing our marketing message to those customers. We're continuing to refine it and get more narrow as we progress and learn more about our customers.

Rapid Growth Driver 3 — Right Business Model

Bringing on an investor was a major change that really laid the foundation for growth. Having already bought out my business partner, I couldn't put more of my personal assets at risk — I had only my hard work to contribute. And if you're not going to put your own assets at risk, then you grow slower. So that's helped with growth.

We've also brought on an American partner. Again, a slight change in business model to give someone who works in the business alignment in growing the business, by having them behave like a business owner. A lot of the thinking that I've done around the business model is recognising that we're a service business at the moment, but we're transitioning to a product business.

Rapid Growth Driver 4 — Sales Focus

We've implemented a weekly sales update from the team done by video (because we're a remote team). So the key metric is monthly recurring revenue, which demonstrates customer acquisition but also if we've lost anyone (churn). We report on that on a weekly basis, and sales do a video about that and talk about new customers or lessons learned if we've lost someone. That keeps everyone in the sales team focused on trying to increase our MRI.

I've learned you need to have an offer — you can market all you want, but if you're not presenting an offer that encourages someone to buy, you're not giving them the option to say, 'Yes'!

In our email signature, we offer a Xero 'health check' and a Xero 'setup', for example. We make little changes like that so we're presenting an offer and we give them the option of saying yes, rather than just providing information.

Also, I'd been doing account management in a very ad hoc way. Our sales guy was an accountant, not a trained salesperson. Again we had just taught ourselves sales — we didn't have a lot of structure around how to do sales or account management, or making sure that our portfolio of clients was happy.

I had some great discussions with the Build Live Give community about documenting standard operating procedures. We were trying to train account managers on the team, and it wasn't something that I had done. We didn't have a documented procedure about how they could do the role well, what was expected of them, how often they should be setting up the check-in calls, what kind of reminders they needed in their calendar, and what they should discuss in these check-in calls. There was a whole lot of missing information because our processes had been very ad hoc. Creating that documentation really helped. Now we have three account managers. They're still learning the role, and documenting some processes meant we could transition people into this important role.

Rapid Growth Driver 5 — High-Performing Teams

The types of people we've recruited in the last year are different from the type of people we recruited in the first year. To hire great people, we pay them a little more than average because a great person can do ten times the amount of the average person.

More specifically, we've been working on career plans for the key staff in the business. We will be rolling those plans out to everyone. We have a holistic conversation about what they want out of their career and their personal life, and then together, we map out how we can achieve that and what type of training and experience they need. We look at whether they need to be rotated into another kind of business.

Then we know all of the decisions we make around training courses align with their goal, and with Bean Ninja's goals. And at Bean Ninja, we've had quite a few discussions about how to create career development plans and types of training, such as on-the-job, external and internal training. That has helped me shape our internal development plans to build team members. It is one reason we've got really high staff retention rates.

Live

With all the changes I made over the past 12 months or so, changes have occurred from a lifestyle point of view. This is what Build, Live, Give is all about.

In the past three years since I started the business, I only had two weeks off completely for a holiday. By creating systems, gradually setting up the business to run without me, I've been able to schedule another week holiday and, going forward, to take far more holidays.

In the meantime, even though it's hard for me to take more than a couple of days off at a time, I still have a good lifestyle. I go surfing and get to family events. Even though I work a lot of hours, my lifestyle is flexible, so I can always be there for important events outside of work.

I've made a lot of big decisions through the last 12 months, both personal and work. I've fixed the operating procedures, and now I am driving sales. I am launching a podcast. I am also looking at launching the online courses and other ways to make the business less reliant upon me.

Because I am putting my family and home first, and finding space for myself, I am more at peace. I focus on the big-ticket items that are going to move the needle, rather than just focusing on the small day-to-day.

Having good people around me in the Build Live Give community gives me the confidence to make big decisions. I know I'm not missing something important. The risk with big decisions is that it can come back to bite you if you neglect something. So it's great having a good network of people around and being able to discuss things with Paul.

Give

The main way that I give back at the moment is to my team, my family and my partner.

I had to make sure I had enough time and attention to my family and my partner. After that, my next focus is on helping my team live great lives. That means making sure they earn enough but also that they've got flexibility, they're happy, they have rewarding work, and they have opportunities to travel. And that's been my focus in the last year. I'm trying to give the best life that I can to all of my team, and then we try to give back to clients too.

Previously, I have just donated to a charity, and I do support Opportunity International. But I feel the biggest contribution I make is to help my team live happy, rewarding lives.

I am also helping entrepreneurs make a positive change in the world. If I look back at that sliding moment where I could have stayed in my job in Brisbane Airport and continued to work those long hours, and sum up how I feel about my current situation — it's played out perfectly.

I love what I do, and so I don't mind putting in extra hours to build an asset that's my own. Working with a team that I like, doing work that I find interesting, I know I made the right choice. I've found my calling.

I love being an entrepreneur. I just love business. Every day I wake up and feel, this is interesting, different, challenging and playing to my strengths. I was a good accountant. I kind of enjoyed it, but I didn't wake up excited about it every day.

Build Live Give Nick Baldo

My solopreneur story

I started working for a consulting firm right out of college. I was excited about it because, as a consultant, I didn't really know what I'd be doing. That came true. I got to work with many different clients. Pretty quickly, it dawned on me that this wouldn't be my long-term career. I had to travel a lot. There was a lot of bureaucracy. It is a big corporation, I didn't feel it was innovative, and I started to think that there was more out there for me. I quickly identified that I would like to escape at some point. Within a couple of years, I got into books on real estate — investing and flipping houses here in the United States.

A couple of years into my job I went part-time. Within four years, I left my corporate job to do investing full-time. Since then my business has taken many twists and turns. That was about four years ago.

Then I faced a key challenge: I want to do a lot and have a lot of ideas, but sometimes I'm just throwing darts. I don't know what to focus on or how much effort to put into things. I was really challenged about knowing where to spend my time. I knew I was talented and had valuable assets. I just wasn't sure who to contact.

I thought Build Live Give could potentially solve that for me. I'd heard a lot of good advice in the Build Live Give podcasts, and I knew I wasn't currently surrounding myself with talented, smart people. I wasn't being challenged to lift my game. I was stagnant.

Build Live Give provided a forum to meet really smart people in industries that are similar to mine, explore different techniques and strategies, and to learn from others' experiences. At the same time, I could share my experience.

Build

Rapid Growth Driver 1 — Personal Effectiveness

I'm embracing the idea of a Virtual Assistant. I was extremely reluctant to take the step of hiring a Virtual Assistant. I saw it as a cost. But that has been one of the most successful things I've done. I now embrace having an assistant to do the tasks that don't make me money, or that are repetitive or not value-added tasks. Being able to trust somebody with that is a great experience, not only from an effectiveness point of view but from the standpoint of teaching me to let go and trust others with the work I was holding so tightly to myself.

I tried hiring one myself, and that did not work out, so I used The Virtual Hub[1], which is one of the Build Live Give recommended providers. The assistant I got was trained already, they had standard tools that they use, and I didn't need to teach them the effectiveness tools we use. Also, I pay for a block of hours. And for me, that was a cost saver. When I had an hourly Virtual Assistant, I would find myself thinking, *'I won't give that task to them because that is another hour I'll have to pay for.'* I pay my VA for the block, and you know you're paying for that block no matter if you use it or not. It pushed me to find more for the VA to do to make them productive and fill that time. It's been great.

Rapid Growth Driver 2 — Ideal Client

The biggest revelation I had was that not every client is a perfect client, nor is every client a client worth having. In the initial stages of entrepreneurship, any revenue seems to be good revenue, and maybe hustling OK as you're starting out. You want to get money through the door. But I realised some clients take too much time and some are not aligned with my values. They are the ones I shouldn't be pursuing. In Build Live Give, speaking with others in the group, I started to learn that identifying the ideal client means that you can fulfil what they want. I built processes to identify what the perfect client means to me. It's been difficult, but it's been really good to learn how to say no to some and embrace others.

---

1   https://www.thevirtualhub.com

Rapid Growth Driver 3 — Right Business Model

I am taking a more creative approach to bring money in the door. The industries I'm in are traditional, and there is nothing new or exciting about what the business does. I'm finding ways to add on products and services that other competitors don't have and ways to differentiate my business from others in the industry. I'm making this business more 21st century and customer-service focused. That has been really great as far as bringing more revenue.

One of my businesses is an offshoot of my real estate investing, which is our home-improvement business — home renovations. So far, we have used a standard model — our renovator finds out the client wants to pay and we do the work. We are experimenting with a subscription-based model for continuous work, selling hours for our carpenter or other skilled tradies so that we can have recurring revenue in an industry that almost never sees that. That's something we're working on.

Rapid Growth Driver 4 — Sales Focus

This ties back to my ideal client. I've been focused on prequalification of our customers and the idea that you want to spend a lot of time on sales, but you want to be spending a lot of time on sales with the customers that are best for you. The Build Live Give community spawned a process I use for qualifying customers and identifying those questions we can ask upfront so that we're not wasting time with customers who are not right for us before we spend time going to site visits and doing face-to-face meetings. I identify as quickly as possible whether this is not our ideal client and move on to the next.

Rapid Growth Driver 5 — High-Performing Teams

Traditionally, in my industry, people are not excited about technology. But I still find it extremely important to focus on processes for my team members and to document these processes. I make a 'playbook' or a 'roadmap' for the different things we do — whether it's my employees logging their time, submitting receipts, or even managing the project and communicating with clients. I found that the more we document upfront about how we're doing things as a business, the better results we get. And the more consistent our product is for our customers.

Live

I was travelling a lot when I worked in corporate, but it wasn't fun travel. I went to South Africa, and I thought, 'Wow, this would be a great trip if I was with the people I love and not working on something I wasn't passionate about.'

More recently, my wife and I are travelling together, and that's a passion of ours. We have had five really big trips in the last year. And we love exploring new cultures, new places. The time I have with the people I care about has increased significantly. I'm on my own timeline — still highly motivated, still working really hard — but I am making those decisions with my family in mind. That's been really great for all my relationships.

Give

What is nice is that when my revenue and income go up, I feel more comfortable with charitable donations. That's something my wife and I have started to do a little bit more in our community. We support pet rescue animals in our area. We are pet lovers ourselves, so we have been investing a bit in the various organisations in our area who can help with that. It is so nice to do it without worrying about pinching pennies. Build Live Give means we've been able to increase our revenue and our income so we can feel a lot more comfortable about that and give back.

Summary

Leaving the safety of your job to start your own business is a brave decision. Only when you've done it yourself do you know how hard it is.

You should congratulate yourself for making a decision that a lot of people think about but never make. You will need the new skills I've talked about throughout this book — and a supportive peer group like the Build Live Give community — to overcome the challenges that you'll face.

Here's a reminder of the essentials we have addressed in this book:

1. Rethink time — more hours in the day is not the solution to your challenges. What matters is *how* you spend time. Get a Virtual Assistant and use the right technology to eliminate your time challenges and focus on the tasks that only you can solve

2. Identify your ideal client — niche down. The quality of referrals is a good indication if you have this right. Have a hypothesis, talk to clients and participate in social media groups to prove or disprove your assumptions. This is ever-changing

3. Choose the right business model, so you work smarter and not harder, and start paying yourself to fund your lifestyle

4. Focus on sales. Create an offer that converts. Up to the first USD $1 million, it is in your hands to generate leads and convert them. In saying this, there are parts you can delegate

5. Once you create momentum and win lots of clients, you can build a high-performing team. This will give you a business, not just a job.

Focus on the Five Rapid Growth Drivers and build a business to fund a lifestyle and give back.

So, how's life looking now?

I know that running your own business is one of the hardest paths on the planet. According to the Small Business Association (SBA), 50% of small businesses fail by year five. I want to help improve these stats. If these were road death tolls, we would not accept it.

This book gives you a pathway and actions to follow, to avoid the failure that could send you back to a job. By implementing the Five Rapid Growth Drivers outlined in this book, it provides you with the opportunity to live a lifestyle you deserve and to add value to others.

There's a wonderful freedom that comes from living life on your own terms.

If the school calls you to pick up your sick children, this is easy to manage. Spending time travelling with family and friends is wonderful. Spending time with your ageing parents is deeply rewarding. A lifestyle that fits around work — not the other way around — is life-changing.

Creating a recurring income from doing what you love and what you are passionate about is so fulfilling. Catching those dreaded 6 am flights or waking up in a hotel and wondering what city you're in is a thing of the past.

Build an asset that will create wealth for you and future generations.

Common wisdom once spoke about how having a job was safe. But today, the number of redundancies and 'downsizing' make it far riskiest than before. The pressure and the stress this situation causes is draining on all people involved.

Working as a solopreneur puts you in control of your destiny. There is a direct reward for the effort you put in.

Leveraging the knowledge given in this book provides a roadmap for staying in control. Work from anywhere in the world share knowledge with people who generally care about what is done for them. Leaving a positive impact on the world is life-changing.

No silver bullets

This is a proven system, but it takes work. There are no silver bullets, no instant solutions. Systematically implementing the actions from each of the chapters will increase the chances of success. What brought success in a past life will not necessarily bring success in solopreneurship. Instead, the openness to learn and make changes is so important to achieving results as a solopreneur.

So many times I see a business stumble, not because of the market opportunity or service, but because the solopreneur could not get out of their own way to let the business grow. The pace of change makes many feel vulnerable. This is all part of it. We need a little humility to become learners again. Don't do what I did — try to solve it by myself and suffer for too long!

This is not a book to just read once and magically change your life in a flash (is there any such book?). I wish it was that simple.

I encourage you to complete the exercises and do the actions.

There will be setbacks along the journey. It's rarely a linear path. The good news is that this doesn't have to be done alone.

When I left Coca-Cola in 2011, there were several communities for startups and entrepreneurs. They were too many steps ahead of where I was at or they had different goals and were making sacrifices that I was not willing to make.

I was mentored by a 29-year-old who exited his business to Time Warner. He was well-versed in the art of startup land and gave me a deep insight into the sacrifices many of my peers had made. We decided this was not going to be for me, as family and health were more important to me than wealth. This is not the case for everyone and each to their own.

I could not find a community for people who were in my stage in life and had similar values.

This is why I created Build Live Give.

If you would like to know more about how the Build Live Give community can support you, please visit www.buildlivegive.com.

We can help solve some of the typical barriers to results, such as:

▶ Letting go

▶ Sunk costs

▶ Spending

▶ Rejection

▶ Charging for your knowledge

▶ Fear

i. Letting go

Letting go is so important to growth. In a past job, there was a team of trusted people to delegate to. Now, as a solopreneur, there is a push to doing everything yourself. When things aren't working, we default to the old mantra: 'I can't afford to get anyone else to do it, I might as well just do it myself.'

But a solopreneur's ability to overcome this will have a dramatic impact on their ability to be successful. When people work on their own, they can think, 'By the time I train someone else, it's just quicker if I do it myself', and 'No-one can do it as well as me.'

What I say is progress is better than perfection. Let go and realise that other people may not do that task as well as you, but the time you gain to work on the Five Rapid Growth Drivers is time well-spent.

The math is straightforward. If you are paid $100 an hour and a VA is paid $14 an hour, any task you are both capable of doing should be done by a VA. Just because you can do something, doesn't mean you should.

A strength overplayed can become a weakness, as discussed in Chapter 6. Just because you can edit videos, or design graphics in Canva or update your website, that is not the reason to do it. Other people can do this for you, so you can focus on marketing, sales, clients and research — as examples. Tasks only you can do.

ii. Sunk costs

Another obstacle many solopreneurs encounters is the 'sunk-cost' phenomenon. For example, you spend $10,000 on creating a sales funnel which is meant to get results. It doesn't, but because you have spent this amount of money you are not willing to change it. It is obvious to your mentor; it is not working. This is backed up by Google Analytics data; however, a client might say, 'Hang on, Paul, I've already spent $10,000. I don't have any more money to fix it.'

I accept you dropped a large spend on it, but if it waddles and quacks, it is probably a duck. If the funnel is not working, there needs to be change.

iii. Spending

Most solopreneurs have a desire to fund growth through clients paying for services — I get it. You don't want to risk your savings or, in some cases, you don't have access to your savings.

I recommend having a 12-month runway when setting up your business. This takes off the pressure of having to say no to spending money on areas that will have a high payback down the track.

I invested $50,000 from my personal savings into my first business to fund a coach, accounting services, legal, marketing, website, training, etc.

They were the right areas to spend money in. What I didn't always get right was spending it on the right experts.

This is why I have collected vetted experts from around the world who serve solopreneurs like you, to reduce the risk of getting the wrong advice and wasting time in finding someone who is good.

Coming from a job, especially large corporations, the sophistication and infrastructure people are used to is not often found in many experts. I was burnt to the tune of $100,000 over the course of the first five years.

I make sure that anyone I recommend to members has already worked with the Build Live Give community and achieved results.

iv. Rejection

Solopreneurs face rejection on a daily basis.

When you sell your idea, it is like your baby. It's really hard to divorce yourself from a NO.

You become so invested that when a client says no to your offer, you feel like they're saying no to you personally. This can result in a loss of confidence.

Removing the emotion is easier said than done. However, step into the shoes of the prospect and see it from their point of view. This is about them, not you.

Behind every no is a step towards a yes. I don't like the saying; however, it is a numbers game. People aren't saying no to the solopreneur; they're just saying no to the solution presented to get them a result.

Implementing the learnings from Chapter 7 on sales focus will reduce this pain.

v. Charging for your knowledge

Most solopreneurs, including myself, at some point, gave away a lot of work for free. It's a challenge to change internal beliefs on one's worth and charge for knowledge.

The default position for many prospects is to gain as much knowledge as they can for free. This is fair game. The onus is upon you to set boundaries and say no to giving away your knowledge for free.

vi. Fear

The self-doubt we have as humans can never be underestimated. The fears and the demons faced as a solopreneur run deep. I will never forget the first networking event I attended where someone asked me what I did. I started to sweat, and the fear took over.

I had left a senior role at Coca-Cola to do what? I was not sure how to explain it to the person asking me. I went home convinced I had made the wrong choice. Fear is a normal reaction to doing something new. As a solopreneur, it is all new. I heard recently on a podcast that fear and excitement come from the same chemical reaction in the brain. When I feel fear, I tell myself I am excited.

Hearing how other community members have gone through the exact fear they faced reassures you it will pass.

Don't do it alone

There's nothing stopping solopreneurs from taking the true meaning of the term and doing it alone. This book will give you the knowledge to Do It Yourself (DIY).

Simply by reading this book and implementing the exercises, people can succeed. If this has helped you in your journey to do this, I am very happy for you.

If you are uncertain if you want to go alone and would like some help, let's talk to see if the Build Live Give community is right for you, https://buildlivegive.com/more-leads

There's an African proverb that says, 'You can go faster alone, but if you want to go far, you go together.'

Take action

When writing this book, I had hoped to inspire people who:

- ▶ Are unhappy with their current career and would like to start their own business
- ▶ Are brave enough to make the bold leap into solopreneurship but have found themselves treading water, realising it can't go on, and wanting to go to the next level
- ▶ Are well on their way to leaving a legacy for future generations and are now more inspired

One of the reasons for successfully coming through my kidney transplant was my determination to do everything the doctors asked of me. Having the time to work from home and manage my condition made this easier. If I was still in corporate, the result might have been different.

Did I make the same amount of money? No way. Did I protect my most important asset — my health? Hell yeah.

As they say, money can't buy happiness.

I hear many of my fellow transplant patients complain about the boredom and frustration of not working during their condition. It is less about the money and more about the satisfaction of achievement. Less of an issue for me, as I can work anywhere at any time.

In some ways, it was easier for me to leave as I had a burning platform — my health.

Regardless of your reason to be a solopreneur, take the knowledge gained here and make every post a winner.

Chapter 10
LIVE and GIVE

At the start of the book, I mentioned this book was the first of three:

1. BUILD
2. LIVE
3. GIVE

Life is rarely sequential, and I am not suggesting to wait until you have read all three to BUILD, LIVE and GIVE.

I have given many examples throughout the book of living and giving.

So why write three books when I could have combined it into one?

I am sadistic... Only joking!

I believe in:

▸ DO
▸ LEARN
▸ TEACH

I have spent so much time over the last eight years establishing my business while living through my health challenges that I have not made the living I would like.

I want to travel more and learn about how to better invest my money and how to maximise my health, etc.

So, in short, I don't believe I am ready to teach LIVE and GIVE.

I will love to hear from you if you are further down the track than me. I will combine your learnings into the next two books.

The Five Rapid Growth Drivers are business orientated. I will be coming up with another five each for live and give.

If you liked this book and want to continue your journey with me, please go to https://buildlivegive.com/blog/, and you can follow my journey of writing the next book.

I will share the behind the scenes so you can learn how to write a book, while also learning different techniques to LIVE a great life.

— Michelle

D   info. — Melisa

About the Author

(401) 487 1715 Alice, I knew you are up

Corporate Director turned Solopreneur Paul Higgins knows better than most what it is like to struggle at running your own business. Paul refers to people like him as 'solopreneurs' in the book. This doesn't mean you don't have people in your team or people who help you. It does mean that your skills and experience are the driving forces behind you making revenue. Without you, the business would not thrive.

Paul has been mentoring fellow solopreneurs since he left his career in 2011. He has accumulated a wealth of practical experience and skills, which he shares openly in this book.

Paul does all of this whilst living with a condition called Polycystic Kidney Disease (PKD). This condition inspires him to run Build Live Give. On the 28th of February 2019, he had a successful kidney transplant from his best mate (friend for non-Australians). All is going well. Paul believes his condition and personal circumstances have made him the person he is today.

The lessons learnt from his journey can be applied to solopreneurs.

40 Vit C
emerson
$10 → $20   Ortho molecular
Home   Public
*   protocol*
set up account   Stripe
35%   pann info